BEYOND WORDS

QHS RESOURCES FOR LEARNING

Beth Collier

BEYOND WORDS
Prayer as a way of life

First published 1987

Triangle
SPCK
Holy Trinity Church
Marylebone Road
London NW1 4DU

British Library Cataloguing in Publication Data available

ISBN 0 281 04310 8

Photoset by Inforum Ltd, Portsmouth
Printed in Great Britain by
Hazell, Watson & Viney Limited
Member of the BPCC Group
Aylesbury, Bucks

*To my family, who continued to love me
through all the difficult times.*

*And to a hospital consultant
who encouraged me to apply my own character
to the management of illness
and eventual better health.*

ACKNOWLEDGEMENTS

Material from The Alternative Service Book 1980 is reproduced with permission. The Gloria and Magnificat are copyright © the International Consultation on English Texts. The Collect for Epiphany is copyright © The Central Board of Finance of the Church of England.

The extract from 'O Christ, to whom our joy is given', tr. Laurence Housman (1865–1959), is from the *English Hymnal* and reprinted by permission of Oxford University Press.

Bible quotations are from the Revised Standard Version of the Bible, copyrighted 1946, 1952 © 1971, 1973 by the Division of Christian Education of the National Council of the Churches of Christ in the USA, and are used by permission.

The poem 'The Guarding of the God of Life' is from *Poems of the Western Highlanders*, ed. G.R.D. McLean, published by SPCK, 1961.

CONTENTS

1

INTRODUCTION – THE PATH OF PRAYER

Whenever human beings form themselves into special societies and groups they tend to become distinctive in some way. Costume, literature and language are just three of the ways this may happen. Sometimes it is a deliberate attempt to separate themselves from the mass of those outside the special group, but often it is something that develops gradually and almost imperceptibly. Unfortunately these developments have two sides to them for while they serve to keep the group together, they also very firmly exclude other people.

The churches are a good example of this type of evolution of a special society. Over the centuries, the original intention has been overlaid and refined to a point where real barriers are perceived by the 'outsider'. One of the main barriers is the language and vocabulary which now contains so many scholarly, technical and devout words, that it is very difficult for the ordinary person outside the church society to break through to membership, or even to begin to make contact.

Two of these words are 'meditation' and 'contemplation'. The dictionary defines 'meditation' as the 'act of deep thought, the revolving of ideas in the mind'; and 'contemplation' as a 'meditative condition of the mind, attentive viewing and consideration' and goes on to say that a contemplator is a student. The ability to turn ideas over in the mind and to think deeply are two gifts that most of us exercise regularly in our ordinary lives, and by extending the amount of time we spend doing this we can begin to make a mental space for God to enter. We are all, surely, students of life, and being willing to go on learning in our spiritual lives is as important as developing our physical and mental skills.

Many of us, when we reach adulthood, stop developing our inner lives because we think that we have now arrived at what we have been working for during our growing years. Try, instead, to see those early years as training for something you may be ready to take on when you are mature. In your maturity you may then be content to let your spiritual life chug along with the rest of your existence; or you may feel that now you are ready for something deeper and more demanding. This book is intended to help you explore the second possibility, and to encourage you and give you the determination to break through the man-made barriers, because God is inviting you to a spiritually richer life with him.

Contemplation can be an exercise of appreciation and deeper understanding not only of God, but of other human beings. Do not allow yourself to be discouraged by the seeming specialness of Church society with all its obvious and identifiable attributes and symbols, for there is much that goes on in a quieter, less easily recognised form. It is possible to be a contemplative, or deep thinker, even if you do not find any of the established churches very congenial or are prevented, by illness or other circumstances, from attending church regularly. Being a good listener to God is part of contemplation and meditation; so why not see if you are being called to this life style? It does not mean giving up your home and family and going into a special place of seclusion. Extraordinary things can happen to very ordinary people, and it is, perhaps, your ordinariness which is most

2

useful to God. Do not be ashamed of your style of life, for God can change and enhance it and change your perceptions and expectations.

My own way to a new life in God's service was the chance given me by severe, restricting illness and many of the experiences in this book are taken from my own life or the lives of people I have met. They are based mostly in traditions with which I am familiar but there are, of course, many other equally valid sources and responses to Christ.

We can all gain encouragement on our way from the experiences of others, and these help to keep our own efforts and importance in perspective. It is useful to look at the lives of others, as long as we do not lose sight of our own personalities. If we become too involved with someone we admire there is a danger that they become the object of our worship and we fail to discover our own potential.

Here I would like to mention a few people, from the past and the present day, who have walked the path of contemplative prayer and whose lives have influenced me. Possibly they will help you, too, to see people you know in a diferent light and be encouraged if your own situation seems to be a hopeless one for drawing close to God. The people I have chosen are all very different, but they share a common thread of prayerful devotion to God.

PATHS BEFORE US

Julian of Norwich

Dame Julian, sometimes called Mother Julian, lived in the fourteenth century. When she was in her mid thirties, after an almost fatal illness, she experienced a series of visions and revelations after which she spoke and wrote of some of the most profound mysteries of God. Her depth of understanding and her perception in theological matters marked her as an outstanding woman of her day; but there was also a gentleness and attractiveness about her writing that makes it acceptable to ordinary people.

The second half of Dame Julian's life was spent living as a recluse. Her physical life was probably sustained by donations from public funds that were available to support such holy people. A number of people also left her money when they died so she was able to live a simple life of writing and prayer and, perhaps, counselling those who came to consult her, rather than a rigorously abstemious one such as was practised by some of that generation.

In Dame Julian's time there were many hermits and recluses adopting various ways of living. She was not a member of an enclosed order; rather, she enclosed herself within her own house and garden, which was near a church attached to a Benedictine community. Although her writings are typical of the style of the literature of her times, they still have great value for us today because she had the ability to put very beautiful, deep truths into a form for meditation.

Brother Lawrence

You will find a number of references in this book to Brother Lawrence and his very down-to-earth wisdom. Born in the seventeenth century, Lawrence was from a poor family and made his way in the world as best he could, including being a soldier, until he joined the Carmelites as a lay brother. He was put to work in the kitchens and he saw his life as one of labour for God. Even in the hurry and bustle of preparing food for many people, Lawrence retained a calm and loving character. He was constantly judging whether he worked well and whether he had been kindly or otherwise towards others. If he saw the slightest evidence of impatience or other unchristian behaviour he expressed his sorrow to God and then contentedly continued his life, assured of God's unfailing love and understanding.

Brother Lawrence saw every minute of his day as being an opportunity for God to work through him, and he became a source of comfort and sound advice to others. He was able to accept his human condition and yet remain cheerful because he was aware of God working out a purpose in his life. Much has been written about Brother Lawrence and it could be rewarding to read about him further if you feel that your ordinary occupations prevent you from having time with God.

Florence

Florence is the name I shall use for a woman who died only a few years ago. From a stormy domestic atmosphere she emerged to follow a commercial career and later, after nursing her dying mother, became a missionary teacher. Her local church and then a wider province played a large part in her life and although Florence never married, she was 'aunt' and friend to many people in her own country and overseas.

As her faith increased, Florence saw a purpose in her love of music and was unstinting in the contribution she made to congregations and small groups to enable them to enrich their worship, even travelling many miles in bad weather. Her highly developed skills in all forms of needlework were also put to the church's service, not only in producing items for use in church but in passing on those skills, especially to those for whom 'make do and mend' was a necessity. Florence befriended many young women and their families and wherever she travelled she offered kindly help and unobtrusive counsel. She was able to share her time and skills in such a way that no one felt patronised or under-valued. For herself, Florence wanted very little except to know that she was doing God's work and showing his life in all that she did. Her diet and clothes were plain and simple; her Bible and prayer book were well worn and she had an intelligent understanding of them and her faith. Whenever she could, wherever she was, Florence attended regularly early morning and evening services. Her life was an encouragement to those who had to struggle with difficult conditions, for when she smiled, the joy of serving Jesus Christ shone out and made things easier for them to bear.

PATHS BESIDE US

George

George is a retired miner and his hard, dangerous working life has given him a view of humanity and of God that is denied to most of us. Working in constricted and hazardous conditions, George became very much aware of the power of God and the sustaining strength of prayer. The unpredictable nature of his working surroundings and the evidence of the accident figures, helped him to realise how ready he must always be for death. He has had to come to terms with losing friends and workmates and seeing the ensuing destruction of family life in the small colliery village where he lives.

From all this experience George has learnt to live prayerfully. He is very mindful not only of the might of God but also of his compassion and generosity. Every day has its joy and is another step to closeness with the God whom George has come to love and worship.

Joan

Joan has had to give up a job she enjoyed, outside the home, to become a full time housewife because her mother now lives with her and needs constant care and attention. Joan's husband has worked hard on the shop floor all his life and is now in failing health, so he too needs special care and support. There are times when Joan feels she is almost collapsing under these two major responsibilities in addition to all a housewife normally has to do.

Her life is bearable because of the strong prayer life that goes on almost all the time she is looking after mother, husband and housework. Joan sees the nursing she is at present called on to do as being the privilege of caring for God's children, and without her resignation to prayer and service she would, at times, feel like walking away from that life of heavy burdens.

Secret saints

The fact is that we are surrounded by secret saints NOW. Whether or not your tradition refers to 'saints' in the general way of understanding the word, it is evident that there are many very ordinary people living lives of extraordinary richness, sacrifice and service. There is often little or no outward sign of their special relationship with God, but they derive an immense strength and satisfaction which makes the meanest job a joy because it is seen as part of God's pattern. To be able to be involved in such a work makes the most mundane job a privilege.

2

YOU ARE SPECIAL

Many people nowadays feel that their lives are blighted and pointless. They feel useless in what they see as a successful world. Newspapers, magazines and television are always ready to tell us what the successful wear, eat, live in and do in their spare time. We are told what size we ought to be and what our hair should look like. Even our most intimate lives are surveyed, charted and compared.

All this cult of the 'image' immediately excludes the vast majority of people, and mainly the old, the poor, the sick, the unemployed and all those who feel that there are better things to do in life than spending time and money on hours of preening each week. In fact there are millions, world wide, who are outside the charmed circle of the acquisitive society; but for our purposes we must concentrate on the immediate culture in which we find ourselves.

Perhaps you have already rejected some of the seeming aims and rewards of our industrialised society. So in what other ways are you different? I am sure you can think of many labels you like to apply to identify yourself, in order to mark you out as an individual. Whether you are just beginning your adult life or are at the point where more active days are over, you are probably aware of your strong points and weaknesses. Even if you are unable to do anything more than remember a long life behind you, you can still find yourself called by God for special service. If you are able to pick out a few strong and weak points about yourself, how much more can God identify your qualifications for the job for which he is preparing you. 'Are not two sparrows sold for a penny? And not one of them will fall to the ground without your Father's will. But even the hairs of your head are numbered. Fear not, therefore, you are of more value than many sparrows' (Matthew, 10.29).

THE CALL TO CONTEMPLATIVE LIFE

Sometimes we need to be withdrawn from active service in one area of our lives in order to go into training for another kind of work. But thinking about saying 'yes' to a contemplative way of life does not mean saying farewell to the world and having only a dull future to look forward to. Indeed you may need to be very much aware of what is going on around you. If you feel, through great age or illness or some other reason, unable to cope with the world of today in any close contacts or involvements, God can still use you. He is not calling 'anyone'; he is calling you. You, with your failings and doubtings; you, with your firmly held ideas and strongly individualistic approach to life; or you, with your life seemingly in ruins about you; or you, crumpled and disfigured by illness. God is able to scythe through all the obstacles, and you have to believe him when he chooses you for a particular job. Perhaps it will be at a time when you feel you have the least to offer that God will say, 'Now'.

If you are able to say, 'Yes', God will show you what you have to offer from the specialness of your personality and will support you through your work and doubts. In time, when you look back, you will perhaps see how your various experiences of life have prepared you, and how many odd events have come together, to make sense in the light of your acceptance of this new work.

9

The contemplative life would seem very suitable for the lonely and for those for whom solitude is a large part of their lives, and for those who feel themselves to be alone. It is not, however, only for those who feel either the need to withdraw, or for whom close human contact is only possible with periods of solitude between. Busy people, whose lives take them into constant contact with others, may well need to cultivate some aloneness, to step back into themselves and to explore their own inner life in order to function efficiently and effectively. Letting the mind and the feelings idle for a while, like a car motor ticking over, can help to put life and events into their proper perspective; but far more important can be a combination of this with a programme of directed contemplation and prayer.

For some contemplatives the world of action is the more important, with the prayer life being the back-up, the plugging into base, consciously or unconsciously. For others, the more real world is the life of prayer, with intervals of outgoing being the interruption – even perhaps the disturbance. It is as if there are sorties from the contemplative life into the world of action. Is this really a disturbance? Or is it the necessary parallel to life; the opportunity to live the life that is supported by being a contemplative?

Much of the way you see your own life will depend on your individual circumstances but it could at times be an interesting and useful exercise to decide which aspect of your life seems to be the most important. No doubt the emphasis will change through different experiences, and only you can know when the balance is right. Whichever way you decide, with careful prayer you will find that the quality of your life is changed and charged with a new meaning and energy and forebearance. It is possible to become more in sympathy with others, and so those whom we might find difficult become more bearable.

Sometimes, those who meet a contemplative are aware of a great calm surrounding him or her which can be either a positive thing or a barrier behind which the contemplative seems to stand or retreat. You must, therefore, guard against this aura of remoteness, or your ability to use your contemplative inner life for good in the world will diminish. It may be easier sometimes to be self-indulgent and not go out to meet the challenges in everyday life, but you are called to work in the world – only with an added secret dimension. It must not become a barrier, but a secret back-up, visible to others only as they see you as a person who has an unshake-able calm, good judgement and who is unshockable in the sense that you can be told anything because you are approachable and continue to love despite people's mistakes and failure of faith. You must be seen as a rock: a port in the storm of life. In Matthew 16.18 Jesus spoke of the firmness of a church that is built on a rock: 'the powers of death shall not prevail against it'. This work is given to you, not because you cannot do anything else, but as a positive, challenging and demanding job which will perhaps be a new career.

WHAT IS THE POINT OF CONTEMPLATION?

Here are a few points you might like to think about if you feel you are possibly called to a life of prayer.
1 You will be fulfilling God's plan for you.
2 You will have a greater share in the constant raising of prayer throughout the world.
3 You will have a greater share in the burdens and sad-nesses of the world.
4 You will have a greater share in caring for your fellow human beings.

11

5 You may be the only person asked to pray for a particular person or event.
6 Your prayer might be the lifeline that will keep you going through a difficult patch of your own life.

The lone contemplative has to be very disciplined because there are no set times when he or she is to be active in contemplation or to be devoting time to other activities. There is no bell to say, Now is the time to pray, and no support from a surrounding community also engaged in a similar activity. In other words, there are always distractions; both of the sort that cause the office worker to gaze out of the window, and of the sort that are constantly reshuffling themselves at the backs of our minds for many of our working hours.

A member of a religious order devoted to prayer as its main activity lives a very simple life and has duties to perform in order that the community can function in its chosen pattern, but he or she is insulated from anxiety about finding a job, how to afford to look after the family, and all the general worries of running a household and constantly assessing one's financial, social and business standing and planning for the future. I do not doubt that there are other worries ready to flood in, and the dynamics of groups living together can produce some alarming situations, but the general business of day-to-day living is more or less taken care of.

For a member of a contemplative community even the normal noise made by a quiet family can be irritating and distracting, and this is another factor that points to the resolution and dedication that is necessary for a strong prayer life for someone who is in the world and surrounded by its responsibilities. That is one of the reasons I suggest a slow, easy start to this sort of commitment.

12

You may also question the point of embarking on what seems to be such a contradictory life style against the competition of the world, when there are already hundreds of people able totally to devote themselves to this way of life. Why should we bother at all? It is because we are all such individuals; there seems to be no end to the variations on the human theme that God can produce. With all that variety to choose from, it must be possible to find a very close match to the perfect ideal, necessary for the job God has in mind. That is why you are chosen, and the next person, although outwardly perhaps more capable, more able and more suitable in your eyes, is not the person God chooses for the work he believes is ideally suited to you.

Perhaps we embark on a life of contemplation with little enthusiasm because we feel we are not able to do anything else because of our circumstances. But as we are supporting and perhaps liberating others by our prayers, we shall discover that we are also liberating or are being liberated ourselves. We must recognise the benefit to ourselves and be thankful, not grudgingly, but openly and frankly, that a seemingly useless life has been transformed into something beyond all hopes, dreams and visions. It is not self-glorification but a real joyfulness. Once we have come to this point we can feel the real responsibilities that have been entrusted to us, and it gives our lives new meaning and a solid central theme, whatever may be going on round about us.

For some, the path to this stage lies through illness, and I suppose that being physically confined through illness or disability can approach what I imagine must sometimes be the mental state of those in prison. Of course the surroundings and many other factors are totally different, but there is a similarity in that the day is dictated by others and one is totally dependent on someone else for the simplest things.

Those who endure long term imprisonment must surely have some fantasy, mental or spiritual life, that makes the rest of their existence bearable. It is something to retreat into; something to keep at the back of the mind; so, in a much deeper sense, is the life of prayer.

If prisoners are able to pray at all, it is most probably about their immediate concerns and their families. Is it possible in such a situation to pray for the liberation of others? I do not only mean those imprisoned behind bars, but those enduring other forms of restriction. We are all to some extent prisoners – of our routines, commitments and other people's expectations of us. We can sometimes be imprisoned by our attitudes and behaviour which prevent us from praying and from normal development. It takes an enormous amount of struggle to come out of one's own misery and be generous-hearted for others; but once the first willingness has been shown, the path widens and the lights go on and a guiding hand reaches out.

This can be the way out of the trough of despair. If you have been at the bottom of the pit of misery, the only way now is up. We can help ourselves and each other. When you are feeling miserable, do something for someone else. This idea was put neatly by the eighteenth-century clergyman and wit Sydney Smith, in one of his letters. After suggesting to his friend that he take life just a bit at a time he exorted him to keep as busy as possible. 'Try and do good', he suggested, and 'be firm and constant in the exercise of rational religion'. This was good advice then and it is still good advice two hundred years later.

Your reactions to and ways of using these suggestions in your own life will be different from those of other people because there is no one else quite the same as you. You and your life are special and precious to God. You can offer this specialness for his service.

Here are extracts from two well known hymns which you may find helpful to repeat occasionally, especially if you are just beginning this new style of prayer life.

Take my life and let it be
Consecrated, Lord, to thee.
Take my moments and my days
Let them flow in ceaseless praise.

Take my intellect and use
Every power as thou shalt choose.

*

O let me hear thee speaking
In accents clear and still
Above the storms and passions
The murmurs of self-will.

3

✂ ✂

ARE YOU WHERE YOU WANT TO BE ?

'You must be prepared to be considered a fool by the world, if you want to live a religious life,' wrote Thomas à Kempis in the fourteenth century.

When you find yourself unexpectedly alone, it is sometimes difficult to decide how to plan the day. (Bereavement is a different and difficult experience of loneliness which I shall not attempt to discuss here.) If you have spent some time looking after others and have always been used to planning your day round their needs, the prospect of being able to please yourself for a while can be very attractive. For a day or two it is lovely to be able to sit in the sun or by the fire reading a good book or listening to music. You may enjoy a browse round the shops, and eating when you feel like it; but after a while, the average person needs more shape to the day. Some people who live alone buy a dog so that they are forced to go out for exercise. Others make a point of going to the shops every day, and there are many other 'markers' which we invent for ourselves.

Most likely, if you are looking forward to some time on your own, you will make some plans and perhaps include a few jobs or hobby activities you had not previously had time for. These activities serve, amongst other things, to stretch and make good use of the time, and in the process, help you to feel more satisfied at the end of the day. So it is with the

16

life of prayer. There needs to be some shape if you are not soon to tire of it and give up. You may be able to use regular events around you as markers, or if you are capable of being very disciplined, plan the day from within yourself through a prayer programme that can continue whatever more mundane events you are involved in or surround you. This is, however, best not tried at the beginning, for failure now might discourage you from going on. We each need to plan our days for ourselves, as our commitments vary so much, but here is how two retired people helped to bring shape to their lives.

The first was an elderly man who was interested in his local community but because of age and infirmity had ceased to be a very active church member. He made space for his daily prayers by going up to his room in the early evening and spending some time praying, reading and being quiet with God. He devised this plan for himself because he said that if he left it until bedtime, he was too tired to spend the time and care he felt was right for him, and earlier in the day he was surrounded by people in whose lives he wished to play a part. After his early evening prayer time, the man rejoined his family and this use of his time was an accepted part of the day for all of them.

The other example is an elderly lady who, despite her very poor health, believed in doing her housework first thing in the morning. Then she sat down for a rest, timed to coincide with the morning service on the radio. The readings were carefully followed in her Bible and provided something extra to think about during the rest of the day. After the service, the lady made herself a cup of coffee and then carried on with the rest of the day until another, this time self-imposed, prayer time in the evening.

Now the radio service might not suit you, but you could find a similar device that forces you to be quiet and thoughtful at some time during the morning. Even just stopping for a cup of tea and a read of the paper can give you a moment for prayer too. If you have to snatch a quick cup of coffee at work you may still be able to pause while you drink it, look out of the window and just send a quick 'arrow' prayer, or repeat a phrase of praise or thanksgiving at the first and last sip, or even with every mouthful if you really have the time and discipline.

SUBJECTS FOR PRAYER

You may choose some particular event or person for your special care and attention that day. Let us take, for example, a prisoner of conscience. Some newspapers feature such a prisoner from time to time, or mention is sometimes made of a group or type of person who is imprisoned for their beliefs by a harsh regime somewhere. Sometimes it is helpful to concentrate on a person whose name or picture you have seen, but if this is not possible then you can pray in more general terms, for example: for all such people who are worried about their families; for all who have to endure cold and hunger; for all who have to endure constant questioning or who are denied access to any sort of reading matter. During the day you can try to imagine that person's life and lack of freedom and how they cope with their predicament. Think of their family and friends and their anxiety for the prisoner and how they will manage without him. Perhaps he was the main breadwinner of the family and has taken political action in an attempt to speed up the long-term improvements for the poorer members of his nation.

Do not forget the persecutors and those who must carry out harsh sentences. Think of how they are being warped and misused, and how their view of life must be disfigured by their work and the double life they probably have to lead.

18

Perhaps also they live with the fear that a former prisoner will find them later and take revenge. Perhaps the persecutors also fear rejection by their own community. Such tools of a terrible regime are victims of it in their own way.

It may be that the prisoner was a member of a group; try to imagine the group's distress and the probable fear in which they live. You may like to think of all sorts of gifts that could be given to the group, such as patience, forebearance and determination. Alternatively you could take the name of the prisoner and for each letter in the name, think of a gift. Here is a simple example:

J: joy in small things.
O: opportunities to show God's love.
H: the comfort of the Holy Spirit.
N: ncw ways of serving God made clear.

Once you start to think along these lines there is hardly any limit to the ideas that can come to you.

Now, as this is probably the first time you have done this, go back over your thoughts and as each thought around the central theme comes into your head, say a little prayer about it. Just enough to keep you thinking prayerfully, and enough to keep those people close to God through you. There may be many reasons why the person himself might be unable to pray. He could be in that great pit of despair where the will to try again and climb out evaporates. Imagine his mental suffering compounded by harsh conditions and bad treatment. Perhaps he has never really known God; or if God ever enters his thoughts, he rejects him immediately because the evidence of his life does not seem to point to a God of love. You may feel called to pray particularly over a long time, for a special person. Perhaps you are their only lifeline. Even if you have difficulty remembering the unfamiliar name there are other ways you can identify them to God. Alternatively, you can pray for others in similar circumstances whose names you will probably never know. When you begin to feel comfortable and involved with a specialisation, you can be fairly certain that God has entrusted you with that particular care because of the special understanding you are able to bring to it.

There are of course many ordinary, average people in the world, living what appear to be outwardly unmemorable, unimportant lives, and they need caring for just as much as those in more dramatic circumstances. Perhaps they need more care, because those featured in newspapers are possibly attracting a lot of prayers where the ordinary people are not. We must expect a measure of unexciting routine in our prayer lives just as we do with any other task. With less high profile people you may again pray in general terms and at the same time pick out one or two individuals. People with a certain type of job or particular responsibilities may appeal to you. There may be someone you see every day on the way to work but will most probably never talk to, for whom you feel like praying. At one stage of my life I took a regular bus ride past a house where a bedridden old man could be seen from the top deck of the bus. Sometimes he waved at the passengers and at other times just stared into space. I felt he made a good target for prayer. We can all find someone for whom the addition of our secret prayers could be an enhancement of their lives.

Remember that there is no such thing as 'luck', throwing people together; it is only our lack of knowledge and foresight that makes us unable to see that luck is just part of God's plan, and that there are really no such things as hazard and chance. So if you are beginning to feel that this new way of thinking and seeing in your life is a piece of good luck, it may be worth reconsidering how you view all aspects of your life. With God's help and our co-operation in his personal plan for us, we can to some extent determine and influence our circumstances. Sometimes, the physical place in which we find ourselves confined can be transformed by prayer and a willingness to flourish where we have been planted. If we can tame our human passions so that we become willing to be where God wants us to be, it is possible to be content and fulfilled in that place.

USING ALONENESS

The loneliness that many have to bear can be hard at any time of life, but through a more demanding prayer life it is possible to learn not to be frightened of silence and being alone. I am referring here to being thrown on your own resources, possibly even being proud of how well you cope on your own; being in the position of not having to relate to other people all the time or for most of the time. Positively, we might call it being a free agent; someone who has to be responsible for every aspect of their own lives. In this situation, even if we discount loneliness, there is bound to be an amount of space – even of emptiness if we look really close into our hearts.

A good relationship between human beings does not need to be constantly filled with speech and other noise; so too, a relationship with God can be carried on in silence, but this is the silence of contentment, understanding and comfortableness. Think of being by the fireside with a good friend who just accepts you as you are, and you will have some appreciation of the contentment that can be found in God. Our love for God and our contentment with this sort of relationship can only find true expression in our concern for other human beings, known and unknown. If we do not go on to have contact with others, in some form of another, our contentment in God becomes a selfish, self-indulgent retreat where other members of the human family are not welcome. If we offer our aloneness to God, he in turn offers us much hard work, more interest in life, support in our endeavours and a deeper contentment in him. We are offered something that will more than fill the void in our lives. Those who are restricted by illness may find that the only gifts they can offer God are their time and their silence. Given these by us, God is able to provide understanding and therefore meaning to our confinement, and show us un-ending paths out into the world and its concerns.

Even without illness it is often difficult to find anything better than our silence to offer from our tiredness or busyness for use in his service. With silence there are really no restrictions or boundaries. If you have aloneness im-posed upon you, do not waste time disliking it and poisoning yourself with negative feelings. You have to be there and in that predicament so why not, quite literally, make the best of it, and put it to positive use?

One of the 'consolations' of being a contemplative in the world, is that so many of its temptations eventually lose their power; they can only be recognised in the same way that we notice when it is raining. We acknowledge the presence of the rain but it is not greatly disturbing. In a sense, being more inwardly involved, you have cast off from some of the world; not because you condemn it but because your ener-gies are otherwise utilised.

Drawing closer to our loving parent helps us to have greater judgement and discernment and a willingness to cast aside that which is not pleasing in his sight. A rule to live by might be one offered by Thomas à Kempis: 'Take care that God can be with you in everything you do.' In other words, try to live your life so that it is always pleading to God, so that there is not any part of it of which you need feel ashamed.

However busy our lives, and whatever relationships we establish, eventually we are on our own with our Maker. This is quite a thought when you consider all the care and effort that we lavish on relationships with other people. The more opportunities there are for caring, the more time and energy it is possible to expend in this sort of area, and yet at the very end we are each on our own with God. We are social animals; some of us better at being so than others, but however much we influence each other, for good or ill, at the last we have to account for ourselves as individuals.

Perhaps the times when we feel ourselves to be the most lonely are, in fact, the very moments when we are closest to God because we are experiencing a deep truth that most of us rarely acknowledge or have the opportunity to experience in any other way. We are often afraid to make space for this sort of experience in our everyday lives; it is only in deep aloneness that some of us are able to come face to face with God without the trappings with which we usually surround ourselves. Retreating into aloneness or constantly being alone is like stepping across from one world to another sphere of our existence, rather than stepping back to being out of the world or inward looking. Within that sphere of retreat, cultivated by prayer, the world can press very closely and its cares can be considered; it can be given time but with no fear of our being crushed by it.

Most of us will never be great public figures capable of dramatically changing the world, but we can work away relentlessly in our own corner and make our own patch blossom and flourish. We are able to change our lives and attitudes far more than we might imagine. If we can find the courage, it is possible to decide that *today* is the day which will change my life. There is a saying that has now become very well known: 'Today is the first day of the rest of your life.'

Whether our lives are so busy that we hardly stop to draw breath or whether they seem so empty that the days seem like weeks, we all need to come to terms with our circumstances. There may well be room for some physical improvement, but that does not always affect the way we feel inside our deeper selves. From what I have suggested in this chapter, you may be able to pick out one or two ideas that will help you face your own lifestyle with a fresher and deeper appreciation of its potential or, rather, of your potential within the life you have to live. You may well be able to work towards a greater contentment in the future, or to appreciate more something you have had to live with or endure, without being aware of it.

In turning to a more prayerful way of life it really is possible to make a new start with God in a way that is not always possible with our fellow human beings. Humans may forgive and try to forget, but if they have been, or feel they have been, greatly wronged, their humanity tends to get in the way of making a new relationship successfully. Of course, sometimes a relationship is strengthened by going through a time of anger, doubt and torment whilst relative positions and attitudes are sorted out into a new pattern within the new identity of the commitment, but it is all too easy still to allow the battle scenes to smart and niggle. With God, once he has given forgiveness, the matter is ended; there is no grudge and there really is a clean sheet on which to start again. In our endeavour to live a godly life we must not become judges of our fellow men, for how can we be certain that they are not also engaged in a similar struggle to our own?

Thomas à Kempis put this idea very neatly when he said: 'We are all frail, but you ought to consider none more frail than yourself.'

Up and follow, Christian men
Press through toil and sorrow
Spurn the night of fear, and then
O the glorious morrow.

Yea, let each our hearts prepare
For Christ to come and enter there.

4

SILENCE

The main element in the life of a contemplative is silence. It must be either got used to, if it already exists in your life, or be created and preserved in a noisy world. Both these exercises require determination. I remember hearing a monk speaking about the first few months in his monastery, which he had entered at about twenty years old. For him, the most difficult thing to come to terms with was the loneliness when he was not involved in some corporate activity. Without the usual support of family and friends, he felt adrift and abandoned and, of course, he was not able to leave the monastery in search of friendship, so that time had been a very real agony.

Imposed silence can so easily be misinterpreted as rejection and exclusion, and of course, sometimes it is. Or it may be the leaving alone of a sick person to rest and recuperate. In the case of the permanently disabled, it may be the leaving alone to give them the opportunity to work out a new way of living a life of independence. All this is perhaps strongly contrasted with a time of intense interest and caring such as when a person first becomes ill or disabled, so that the silence afterwards seems particularly empty.

Creating silence in noisy surroundings requires practice but is perfectly possible even in the noisiest place. Putting up a barrier behind which to retreat can be done by deep breathing exercises and relaxation so that our bodies do not notice the disturbances around them. Real concentration can, at first, be encouraged by a formula we have worked out for our personal use in order that we may begin our journey inwards. Some suggestions you could perhaps consider for helping you to relax and concentrate on your prayers or just to enable you to be quiet with God are these. Repeat over and over some short prayer or phrase you have collected for this purpose (see chapter 10). Or visualise a scene you know and love. Perhaps there is somewhere you know that is very peaceful, to which you can travel in your imagination for a brief period of refreshment. It may be helpful to think of yourself walking down a narrow country lane and seeing at the end a wonderful view opening out before you. Perhaps you are one of those people for whom sound is very important. In this case it could be helpful to use this as a way of helping to get yourself into the right frame of mind to be quiet and prayerful. The sounds should be calm or steady or rhythmic, such as the sea, distant sheep, or the wind in the trees.

Two everyday expressions often used are, 'silence is golden' and 'silent as the grave'; but it is hard for those of us who enjoy any degree of hearing to imagine a totally silent world. To be called, or invited, to silence, is a privilege, yet it is often very difficult to find real silence in our present world. Inner silence, or the ability to detach yourself from your surroundings in order to withdraw from distraction, is a necessary part of being a contemplative. Living a contemplative life is sometimes made much more difficult by the fact that we are surrounded by constant noise of one sort or another. Let us, however, assume that you have devised a way of obtaining some relative quiet. Perhaps you are able to go to a certain quiet place or have marked a relatively undisturbed part of the day where you can, possibly with the aid of deep breathing and relaxation, train yourself to concentrate on your prayers and not be so aware of the surrounding noise.

WHAT HAPPENS IN THE SILENCE?

At first, closing the eyes and thus cutting ourselves from visual distractions often leads to increased awareness of sound. Many blind people are able to travel by bus and can be sure of leaving it at the right stop because they are able to distinguish the changing noises as the vehicle passes buildings, open spaces and railings. If, in the silence, you feel overwhelmed by noise that you have not noticed before, it may help if you concentrate on one recurring or continuous noise. This will narrow down the range of sounds you are aware of. For most of us there are other distractions in the silence. We remember jobs we should have done and jobs we have to do. Anxieties crowd in, and sometimes it seems impossible to go on being quiet with so many mental distractions. Perhaps saying a simple prayer will help. Just say something like this:

> Dear God; you know my deepest anxieties and all the responsibilities that surround me in my daily life. Help me, for a few minutes, to put these things aside and be near you in the silence.

Then think again about some of the things that have occurred to you and distracted you. Imagine they are written on the pages of a big book, a page for each concern. As you remember each one, imagine you are turning over a page and when you have reached the end of the list of subjects, imagine having come to the end of the book. In your imagination close the book and put it to one side. Now just say another simple prayer such as: 'Come to my heart, Lord Jesus. There is room in my heart for thee,' or 'Help me, dear

God, to lay my troubles before you and be still in your presence.'

There are occasions when it is easier to be prayerfully silent. Perhaps it would be helpful to concentrate on something like an incident from the Bible or a painting or a piece of sculpture that has a biblical subject or a theme that you find moving or important emotionally. One of my favourite subjects is a small fifteenth-century German carving of the nativity scene. It is such a gentle, human, sympathetic interpretation, as well as being a beautiful piece of art. For me, it works as a good calm point from which to travel into silence. Others may like to use a favourite view, or a plant, or even a piece of music. Whatever you choose, go back to it when you find your mind wandering away to your worries, and with practice it will become easier to concentrate.

There are, of course, times when we take our troubles to God, but the silence I am speaking of is the restorative rest between our human busynesses. There are times when we can travel into deep meditation and others when we hear God speaking to us. At other times there is just silence and we must accept that, as well as the more dramatic occurrences. Often, when we go back to our daily lives after one of these times of withdrawal into silence, our lives seem to have a different perspective, problems assume their proper proportions and we are generally able to cope better. This can happen without any concentration on our anxieties in the silence. During our withdrawal the troubled waters of life have settled and we are able to see more clearly how our feeble efforts might be more constructive.

When we have a problem we are often advised to 'sleep on it', and in the morning things often seem not nearly as bad or as complicated. A period of silence can have a similar effect but, of course, it must be as well as, rather than instead of, where professional help, medical, financial or otherwise, is necessary too. Silence is not an alternative therapy, but an additional one.

Those of us who live in the comparative absence of noise, in the sense that we spend many hours alone each day and do not listen to the radio or meet other people, have a somewhat different experience. It is good to make an effort, if you can, to have some contact with other human beings at least every few days and to keep up an interest in international news; but living a quiet life makes it easier to plan a prayer life.

You should be able to plan periods of special time when you are physically still, and make positive use of the silence between those times, to practice the presence of God. This means thinking, working and moving, prayerfully; being always conscious of God in the small things we usually take for granted. If you have ever suffered a period of ill health and incapacity you will understand more readily what it means to be able to delight in all sorts of simple everyday things that have temporarily been denied to you. How wonderful it can be to get up out of bed and dress oneself! To be able to move stiffened joints; to discover a new way of using your fingers so that you can eat without help. Just to be able to sit in front of a window and feel fresh air on the face is a delight for someone who has experienced living in the dungeon of illness.

Let us hope that you do not have to go through a period of real suffering in order to appreciate some of these simple things. In your quiet moments just imagine, for example, the complicated electrical impulses and muscular responses that must take place in order for you to lift a cup of coffee to your lips and drink – and be thankful. Sometimes, instead of letting your mind idle, like a car ticking over, or allowing it to build up your worries to a frightening level, use it to expand the real world you inhabit.

An easy way to do this, especially if you live a quiet life, is to think about things around you and take your thoughts back to their beginnings and forwards to their ends. There is a pencil on my desk. It could set my thinking back to the forest where the wood came from. I have enjoyed many happy days in the countryside and I might say a little prayer of thanksgiving for those happy times. This can lead me to the forestry workers, and so on to many other concerns. Then I realise that I know very little about the other part of the pencil, the graphite or lead. I may resolve to take the trouble to find out, and thus add to my knowledge of creation.

Next, my thoughts might go to the shop assistant who sells the pencils, and so on to my use of it, and to its end; perhaps being discarded when it has become too small to hold easily. Then I am led to think and pray about the refuse workers and how, eventually, most of our waste is returned to the earth. I like to think that the pencil stub will rot and return nutrients to the earth, but I suppose that might be rather fanciful and I must accept that it will probably end up in a non-biodegradable plastic bag and will still be recognisable many years hence. So I am led to God's wonderful creation, and to prayers and meditation on that subject there is no end.

Try this exercise, prayerfully, next time you have a few quiet minutes and see how the walls of your life are pushed back and how the silence can be used to link you with the world as well as more directly with God.

THE JOURNEY INWARDS

The journey inwards is not to a dark place full of terror but it will almost certainly be through darkness where many obstacles will be encountered, but at the centre is the irresistible light. Like a moth to a light in a darkened room, we are attracted to some aspect of God but the way to that light is often fraught with disappointments and hurtful events. We shall meet all sorts of manifestations of our personalities that we have failed to recognise before, or have brushed aside rather than working through·them. These discoveries are part of the real you, and if you do not work them through, they retain their power and become traps waiting for another occasion.

Enter the darkness with a prayer and keep in your mind the certain knowledge that because the time is now ripe for you to take this part of your journey, God is waiting for you at the other side of the great abyss. His light may be for a time obscured, but it does not go out.

DEALING WITH EVIL

What is evil? We could most easily answer that with some very concrete examples of the manifestations of evil in the world, but we are required to find a more carefully thought out answer. We can keep the reply simple by defining evil as anything that gets in the way of God's purpose. Material things that God would like us to enjoy as part of creation, become evil when they assume a greater part in our lives than is their due. When we make idols of our money or our physical comforts or our ambitions, they are all bricks in a wall we build between ourselves and God. We add to that wall when we give in to our selfishness. We can go some way towards conquering these feelings but it is God's love that supports and allows this.

Hell and the notion of hell as a place of eternal damnation is a somewhat unpopular concept these days; so doing something for fear of being otherwise sent to hell may not weigh heavily with us. Rather, we do things in order to please God or to be more near the perfection he does not expect but does expect us to strive for. We need to have a vision of excellence in order that we may approach a measure of satisfactory endeavour.

Life is sometimes made difficult when we think we see evil working in others or when we feel threatened by what we would identify as evil. In this sort of encounter it is still possible to say a prayer for that person and his distress and predicament. Perhaps there is, in that person, some accentuation of an emotion you have yourself felt at one time but the surrounding events have been such, that the anger, or other destructive feeling, has not bubbled to the surface in a confrontation. This is, perhaps, an extension of the phrase, 'There, but for the grace of God, go I.' Having faced our own evil and removed its blackmailing power, we have to realise that it can still appear in many forms, even in those very close to God. We need to have a plan ready to deal with this possibility and perhaps the simplest is to be open enough with God so that we can offer him the evil, our own reaction to it and the best solution we can visualise. Alternatively we can simply offer the problem and our sense of dilemma to God and a willingness to listen for the way forward to be made clear.

Letting in the bright light of God's love to shine on evil, is often a good way of showing up the shabbiness of wrong-doing, and diluting its effect on either the outer or the inner man and sometimes causing a permanent change for the better. There are times when the apparent harshness of the world is only bearable because of the truth and beauty and richness of the secret inner life, and even the prospect of death is full of promise because of the possibility of a life beyond our human imaginings. There can be no doubt that life can be very, very hard sometimes, so it is essential that the sacred thread of our inner life be kept strong both for our own sake and the sake of all those whom God has entrusted to our care in the way of prayer support.

RECOGNISING OURSELVES

When we begin the journey inwards and strip away the outer trappings of our personality by which the world recognises us, we discover a miserable, cringing, colourless being, underneath. This is the raw material of your new identity. The inner person, so long neglected, is waiting to find life through your resolution to begin working with God rather than against him and his purpose. It is hard to believe that God can love this spineless creature, but it is through his love that each one of us can find our true potential and from that, move on to use the gifts God has so generously given us. This brings to mind one of the 'arrow prayers' that I find helpful to use: 'God be in my heart and in my understanding.' He really can be, if we do not obstruct his way.

Perhaps it is beyond our human comprehension that anyone can be so unfailingly loving and supportive as God is, and that is one reason why we sometimes feel like rejecting him. Our human judgements, from their small overall view, put up barriers between us and God. We must try to be more generous hearted towards one another and more willing to try and understand the eternal sustaining goodness of God.

If we can imagine the stripping away of most of the things that surround our physical lives, we are left without the markers of our worldly existence. Those events and objects that seemed so important, diminish in relevance, and those who have neglected the inner life are left with very little identity and few signposts. What a frightening experience it would be, to be adrift without our worldly props and without a reservoir of inner resources; to have all the strong emotions, good and bad, and not to have a background of training, taming and directing in the way God has planned for each of us. Without our props we perhaps become unrecognisable to others and a problem to ourselves. When this happens, as it may do through illness, severe hardship or some traumatic event, it would be most natural to be miserable and go through a period of mourning for our old selves. But perhaps the closing of this particular door is the opportunity for another to open and we should, in fact, be looking forward rather than back.

The depth of the soul is unfathomable and the possibilities for growth are unimaginable. It is rather like trying to estimate the limits of outer space; whatever conscious effort we make to expand our understanding and define the limits of our tolerance, endeavour and personal possibility, there is always some more left. There are some remote reaches that alone we are not able to penetrate, but God knows them as untapped resources. As we grow in faith, we are often told that God does not give us more than we can bear and that when he calls us to the seemingly impossible, he also provides us with the means for obtaining extra strength and courage. Sometimes the process we go through transforms us and we are surprised at our own endurance, but even after all that, there is still more to us. Of course, we are usually unaware of this as it is only revealed to us when we have most need of it. After even a little despair, how ready we are to accept help, and how good the light of God's love seems.

THE INNER DARKNESS

Our lively imaginations and faithless hysteria, when we are in distress, make us liable to race ahead of events and be overwhelmed by the seeming darkness which awaits us.

God, however, takes us a step at a time. A day at a time is what we are asked to consider and cope with. Sometimes we look ahead and wonder how we can face what we see on the horizon and it is often then that we become too confused and distressed to see what God is offering us now, today, to deal with what is happening this minute. We do not need to know how we shall deal with what is ahead because when the time comes, we shall be given guidance; but it is easier to accept that idea if we get into the habit of walking daily with God so that we really do see his care for us unfolding day by day, unfailingly, although not always in the direction in which our human expectations are looking. It is easier to accept the unexpected if we set before us firm expectations of God's support, rather than always trying to forecast events. A good father does not always say 'yes', and we must accept that what seems to be disappointment, is often for our greater good in a greater plan than our perspective can grasp.

Sometimes the inner journey is like a thriller story where sealed orders are given as each stage is reached, but where only the masterminding boss can see the whole picture and the participants are only expected to follow the orders at each stage and be confident that the whole plan will, in fact, work. We can somehow have an idea that there is a goal, although in our imperfect understanding of the time-scale and methods of God, we find it difficult to help our fellow travellers. The best we can say is, that in our own experience such and such has been the case and might point to *a*, *b*, or *c*, as being the way forward. There is a great temptation, perhaps born out of superstition or a longing for tidiness on a human scale, or a yearning to see the way ahead more clearly, to interpret events and ideas in a way that would seem to tie up a lot of loose ends, as if we were attempting to tidy up God's desk before the holidays. The only thing we can really say here is that we should mind our own business, and not try to justify God's plan in human terms. We can only be sure of an event after it has happened and even then, there is a great deal of room for misinterpretation.

The artist complains that it is impossible to justify art to the ordinary person. We can go on from that to say that it is almost impossible to justify many of the things that worry us, and yet continue to believe in a just and loving God. At some point there needs to be a great leap of faith so that we can accept that it is so, and that in our own particular lives we are given special jobs to do, whether outwardly visible to others or not; whether great earth shaking work, out in the international world or in the confines of a hospital bed, or in everyday routine.

Even mundane jobs, such as the washing up, can be an opportunity for service of the most careful kind, for others, and in the process become an exercise in prayerful action in his service. Such a simple, often irritating, necessity of living can thus become something to look forward to as a time to review our attitudes towards others or a quiet rehearsing of some short rule or words of encouragement that serve as a check in our lives.

If we can come through a time of suffering or darkness or heaviness of spirit, we then have the knowledge that it is possible to survive such an experience and we may even be able to pick out one or two tips that can be useful to other people. Our own survival is in itself a witness, and if we emerge enriched by the experience then we can indeed be useful to God and our fellow men and women.

FINDING YOUR OWN WAY FORWARD

The world recognises us mostly by our outward appearance – or perhaps by our voice on the telephone. Sometimes in reporting a conversation, it is hard always to remember who said what until a listener says 'That sounds like *A*'. This is because that particular remark reflects the person others see us as; but the inner life is only fully recognised by God. Even to ourselves we are often a mystery.

The raw material of our souls might be described as a badly out-of-focus photograph. During our lives and the process of our spiritual growth, we must always be trying to make the picture clearer. It is possible for very radical changes to occur in a life, for any number of reasons, but whatever we do, is always reflected in the growth, or otherwise, of the inner life. To be honest with ourselves is to see the picture as it really is: in the long run this is the simplest way to make real progress because honesty implies not wasting time on superficialities – the nonsense of our image-conscious lives, imposed for the benefit of others.

Those who are called to the life of retreat into some community are often, in effect, saying that not only do they renounce the temptations of the world but also give up the fight they have to make against them. There is a world of difference between being aware of the world and its problems but removing oneself from engagement in physical terms, and attempting to live close to God and somewhat removed from the world mentally and spiritually, though still in a position to be bombarded by and having to encounter the physical challenges of everyday life.

If we see it as being right that we should remain where we are in the world and at the same time want to ask God to use us more fully, we need not fear being overwhelmed by him. He wants our identity to be recognised in his service. It is each one of us, as the individuals he has created, that he wants in his service. It is hard to get the balance right as we strive to see his guiding hand and his love before us, calling us to live in him. If God's only plan was to overwhelm us and take away our will and our identity, then he would have little need of us in the first place. 'Take my life and let it be consecrated, Lord, to thee,' is a plea for transforming, not for swamping. We have all been given a measure of intelligence and judgement, and these faculties are to be put at God's disposal. This part of our identity is to be shaped and enhanced by God, rather than our turning ourselves over to him with the notion that if we just sit back, without making any effort, we shall better serve him.

Just as we can usually recognise our good and bad points, if we take the trouble to think about them for a moment, so we should go a step further and consider what we are willing to bring to a new contract with God. How can our various gifts and strengths be best used? We may need to hunt out a new channel where, through us, God can be enabled to have a greater influence.

Looking for God in others is a part of this new way of life and sometimes, from our limited viewpoint, this is difficult to decipher; so it is important that others see God in us because there may be some inner response that only God will see. For my own part, I would rather there was a slow realisation of the driving force in my life, than a brash bombardment of anyone through anything I might do or say. My own way of sharing the 'good news' is of quiet, indirect appeal, very often unspoken.

Whenever you do a kindness for anyone, do it with an unspoken prayer. You may want to focus the prayer on the action, but if this is not appropriate, then just ask God's protection for that person, or ask that he will realise his own worth or have the courage to let God into his life. Apart from the benefit for the other person, this sort of exercise can often soften our harshest judgement or feelings of disgust. It could well be that this person has been sent to us by God because of the sort of response he knows we are capable of. Let us not forget that we sometimes entertain angels, unawares.

5

⚹⚹

GIVING UP OURSELVES

Something as simple as 'letting go' can be terribly hard to do, however much we may want to hand over the organisation of our lives to someone else. We often notice this when someone faces long-term illness or disability. They spend a great deal of time giving instructions, asking questions and worrying about details. Although I believe we are all very special individuals, I also believe that none of us is indispensable. The style in which our job is done for us in our absence may not be our style, but it is possible it will be done just as efficiently and effectively in a new way.

All our childhood training is geared to making us self reliant, reliable, dependable, responsible members of society. The idea, therefore, of handing ourselves over to someone or something unknown or unprovable in rational, scientific terms, at first seems grossly irresponsible. We sometimes half jokingly say, 'I wish someone else would come and take over, wave a magic wand and get it all organised.' Well, we are not always aware of God's magic wand, but he will support and direct those who will let him into their lives in this new way.

This letting go is, however, a very personal thing and we all need to come to terms with it at our own pace and in our own time. It is counter productive to use overt persuasion, even threats of damnation and the like, in an effort to bring others to this way of thinking. For many, it seems, a season of incapacity, physical, mental or spiritual, is necessary for God to be able to get a word in edgeways. The deep depression and despair that accompany a loss of faith or the shock of having to hand over to someone else our social functioning or our physical care, may prove to be the one moment in our lives when we have time enough, and are desperate enough, to listen. It is a very hard way to come to a simple lifestyle, so perhaps most of us need to make a little time each day to tune in to God and just be still.

I am not supporting the notion that illness is punishment for wrongdoing, either of omission or commission, but only stating that what at first might seem to be the worst thing that ever happened to you, could be the gateway to the best you are capable of; and that best could be far beyond what you believed yourself capable of.

The moment when you turn away from God saying, Why me? What have I done to deserve this? is possibly the moment when you are being specially singled out for new work. If something like this happens to change your life, it may take a great deal of courage to let people see the change.

A man I knew spent the first part of his adult life pouring scorn on the Christian faith and even insisted that 'religion is something you grow out of'. I did not see him for many years and when we next met I was surprised and delighted to find that he and his wife were pillars of their local church. Something had happened in their lives which had brought them to despair and over the brink of worldly ruin, to a feeling of total desertion by most of their former friends and acquaintances. There was only one Person left, and in turning to him they transformed their lives into quiet dignity and joy; in doing so they touched the lives of countless others, myself included. In others there may not be anything akin to the blinding flash on the road to Damascus; but unexpectedly their lives may be touched and transformed

41

into positive living, where joys are found in unexpected places and they can grow to unimagined spiritual stature.

However we are led to it, abandonment, it seems to me, is the first step to fulfilment. We are all usually 'trying too hard', and often getting nowhere. Let us open our eyes to the signposts, and follow our own particular paths home. In the past, some prayerful people have felt that the best way to be close to God was to pray for death; but most of us must realise that there is a great deal to be done before the privilege of being called home.

Two points are raised here: one is that for some, the unmentionable fact of death means giving up in a negative way. For others, it means the opportunity for the positive offering of life and personality, and physical death itself is the gateway to the reward promised to all who believe. For most of us there is a long time to be lived between birth and death, and we have such a narrow perspective that not to abandon oneself to God's gracious care and protection seems rash in the extreme.

There are many reasons why it can be hard to do a very simple act such as going through a gate of commitment. It may help you if you can mark out a day when you will sit down quietly, let go, and ask God to take your life for use in his service. Ask to be shown the way and welcome him into your life. Tell him your doubts and anxieties, and ask for guidance, comfort, or whatever you think you need. Let God be your friend. He already is, but he needs your welcome to be really effective through you. Don't lock him out of your life.

Talking to God in this way will become easier as you go along, and you will feel more comfortable about it. At last you will be able to express your very private and innermost fears and share your joys. Your view of yourself and others will change and you will be surprised by the much more charitable view you have of life and the better judgements you make. You will look forward to using more fully the talents and faculties God has given you. You do not need to keep up appearances with God, so just relax and be yourself.

Here is a breathing exercise which may help you prepare for prayer. If and when you feel comfortable with it, use at any time you feel the need.

Breathe in steadily and say silently: 'Come, come, come, Lord Jesus'.
While you hold your breath, say silently: 'And take my life'.
As you breathe out say silently: 'For use in your service'.

This simple exercise can be used with any other suitable phrase or sentiment and it is a good idea to compile a short list of suitable phrases. The calming effect of a deep breath, or the ability to establish a steady rhythm of breathing can, in itself, help to relax the body; and in the life of a contemplative, it can become an essential aid to leading a fuller prayer life.

ABANDONMENT

Abandoning yourself to God is a hard commitment to make. If you can bring yourself honestly to do it, you will be led through some very testing times when you feel lonely and full of doubt. Go on asking for guidance and repeat your willingness to abandon yourself to God, and later you will find a new freedom in him. Dame Julian of Norwich said, 'We should want to be like our brethren, the saints in heaven, who will nothing but God's will; only then shall we rejoice in God and be content whether he conceals or reveals.'

God needs willing tools for his work and we need to

recognise that without him we are nothing and totally without form or direction. I always keep before me the example of a very old clergyman, beyond the age when he might have expected to retire, who was born and lived all his life in one of the countries of the former British Empire. He had always lived a simple, godly life and when he was asked by his bishop to move away from a parish which he had spent many years building up, to a remote place away from his family and friends, he said, without hesitation, 'Yes'. His friends were saddened by the demands made on such an old man until he explained, 'My bishop is my father in God, and God needs willing hands. It is my duty and my privilege to go'.

Sometimes a prayer of total submission is almost impossible to say, especially if you feel that your obedience may adversely effect other members of your family. But if you do not abandon yourself to God, how else will you find your way and perform your part in his purpose? Half-heartedness has little part in the great plan; for it to work, we must each work through our own part of it. With abandonment comes flexibility and a willingness to work in our own corner without seeing the master plan or the report at the end of the week. It involves an openness to the unexpected and the unusual, and a boldness to do what seems to be right. In all this endeavour we have a first class back-up team – God – and all the thousands of people who are praying for us. Look at, for instance, the form of intercession found in the Anglican communion service; think of how many of the categories mentioned you fit into, and multiply that, if you can, by all the congregations and communities round the globe – all praying for you, as you are for them.

Once you have begun to draw closer to God, do not turn back. Some give up too soon if the way is hard, and turn to worldly comforts, but we should take the challenge seriously. Thessalonians 5.8–11: 'Let us be sober and put on the breastplate of faith and love and for a helmet, the hope of salvation.'

Like housework and cooking, there is no end to this job! You can bake a cake with great care and possibly, love, and it can all be gone in a few minutes; likewise there is always the week's washing and dusting to be done. So it is with prayer. It is impossible to produce an equation of effort multiplied by time to equal a result. Perhaps the word 'result' is in any case too final a concept. What we see as results are just pieces of the kaleidoscope of life forming the part of the pattern that is needed for the moment; the next moment is served by another complicated pattern, the production of which has been helped by our efforts of prayer and care.

WHEN PRAYER IS NOT ANSWERED

What measuring scale is there for knowing when prayers are answered? It is like making a cake without weighing the ingredients – as far as we are concerned, there is no measuring scale because we cannot see the larger purposes of God. Being a contemplative is, perhaps, a thankless task; which is a glib way of saying that we are rarely able to see the answers to our prayers, especially if we have chosen to concentrate them on an obscure area, either geographically or in subject matter. In this case, your work must be taken on trust and faith; sometimes even the most solid faith can be shaken. You have to believe that you are necessary. You have to accept that your particular brief is part of a very large jig-saw, and you may never be aware of any of the other pieces.

If you lose faith, the answer is to go on praying. Your prayers will probably seem feeble and ineffective; but remember, many others have been through this expereince and have been restored to a fuller life of faith. No one would pretend that it is easy, and sometimes total despair seems waiting to flood in, but this is the very moment when those feeble cries for help and guidance and restoration are most badly needed. We do not, however, go back to the place we left, but we find that through the experience we have changed. God's expectations have changed, and we are expected to grow through our experiences and be ready for something different and new. With our horizons widened our view of life has altered.

DEALING WITH DESPAIR

I have already suggested that despair arises partly from being adrift from the usual markers of life so that we are turned in on ourselves. What we then see is often a not very attractive picture of half-truths, deceit and unresolved negative feelings. Against all the things in our innermost selves that make us miserable and ashamed, the good in us seems a very small part; a precious jewel in the murky stream of general human failure. Being very strict with ourselves we might call it sin; and the way to rid ourselves of the burden is to 'acknowledge our wickedness' and seek forgiveness. Then, with ourselves washed clean – and sometimes, if we are full of remorse, forgiveness is hard to accept – we can begin again.

Trying to be good all the time may sound very dull but in fact it can bring great rewards and joy. The inner life of a contemplative requires that we do not become so engrossed in praying for others that we constantly forget to remind ourselves of our need for grace and forgiveness and the forbearance of others, in order to be whole. This endeavour to be good, for want of a better phrase, will reveal itself in our dealings with others, in the care we give to even very small tasks that we attempt to do to the best of our ability. Meticulous attention to detail in the way of being fair, kind, and unwavering on the path that is set before us, will be reflected in our everyday lives.

As human beings we generally work better if we can set some short term goal towards our objective. But with God, we need to be able to 'travel hopefully' rather than insist on arriving. We have to condition and even steel ourselves to accept the fact that we may only rarely see a long-term goal achieved. When we are sorely tried by events, illness or pressures put on us by our own circumstances, some of us may feel like giving up. This could mean abandoning our prayers or, more seriously, our lives.

Those who have been very close to the ultimate step of suicide, know that there is usually a very long period of despair, distress and withdrawal before the brink is reached. Our increased understanding of how the human psyche works tells us that a suicide attempt is not always meant to succeed, but may be a cry for help from someone who sees all other doors slammed in their face. This is not the place to explore the physical, psychological or spiritual realities of this state, but for a person who takes on a prayer load, there is another reason for battling on and seeking help to get over this trauma. Whatever your temporal responsibilities are, you are carrying an extra load of spiritual responsibilities. People's lives have been entrusted to your care. People whom you will probably never meet have their lives bound up in yours, and your life is bound up with similar efforts of others.

Your prayers are helping to make someone else's life bearable, and your life is helping to give meaning to someone else's prayers. How dare you abandon them? How can you find it in your heart to let them down? How can all that is good and best in you, turn your back on the efforts of others.

You know what you invest in your intercessions; just multiply that by the sort of numbers we imagined earlier and understand what a cushion of support you are resting on. Relax, and ask for that support, even though you know you already have it. Ask that all those prayers may have fulfilment in your life rather than your death.

God is the only person you can be totally honest with in times of despair. There is no need to feel shy or stupid. He knows all your weaknesses and worries, but he needs you to admit them and present them to him with humility. Throw away the face you show the world, if it is not an honest face. Discard the pose you keep up and the walls you build between yourself and others. Strip away your preconceived ideas about God so that you can be open to what he wants to reveal to you. Without this load of excess baggage, which we all carry to some degree God can work on the putty we really are. We cannot create matter, only change it, so beside God we are feeble and in need of his support and his overwhelming love. In return, he needs us to be fresh and strong and determined to follow his guidance. He can provide the strength and ideas if we offer him our lives, which are incomplete without his direction, with open hearts and without the false pretences we often show each other.

When God is with us, the most difficult things, such as temptation or hard decisions, seem easier. The person who lives with God is rich, and God never wants to lose us; but we sometimes allow our doubts to overwhelm us and crowd out the influences through which he is trying to reach and comfort us. Thomas à Kempis gave good advice: 'Be humble and peaceable and Jesus will be with thee.'

SUFFERING

If you are suffering, physically, mentally or spiritually, do

48

not ask 'Why?' or 'Why me'? but rather, 'How can I make positive use of this experience'? Suffering helps to put into perspective so many things of this world that get into a muddle or become more important to us than they really are. We lose control of ourselves and have new boundaries given to us; and this is a form of abandonment. Sometimes, to suffer is like looking in a mirror and finding a stranger. We discover good and bad in ourselves, and others see us differently too.

Suffering can serve as a line drawn across our lives. It can be the moment when we have a real choice: to revert to our old selves, to be absorbed by the worst parts of ourselves; or to be transformed by the experience of suffering and blossom into something new that is built on all that is best in us so that we can see the possibilities of continuing to grow and develop in God. Perhaps to take on new responsibilities and be transformed in ways we never had time or opportunity to consider possible.

Suffering, at first, is like being put in prison.

If the suffering involves actual physical pain, there sometimes comes a time when it can be controlled naturally until it becomes only a recognisable sensation and, with practice, this can serve as a reminder to prayer. To live with constant pain can be to live with a constant reminder of the privilege of being always able to approach God.

When the margins of experience and the markers of our daily lives are taken away by suffering and we have arrived at the realisation that we have to rebuild, then sometimes it is possible for great things to happen. It is easy, in the face of terrible, unexpected suffering, to lose one's faith; but God does not go away simply because you no longer believe. He is waiting for you to acknowledge him again at the end of your doubt. He is waiting for you to glimpse him during your suffering. He is supporting you and hoping you will recognise him again. Thomas à Kempis said something that I believe can apply to us very much in the midst of suffering, 'If God will pour into him holy joy, his soul will be full of melody.'

If you are crippled or ill it is often hard to see how you can give your life to God's service – apart from the obvious, physical, difficulties connected with your illness. It is easy to feel 'My life is not my own', and to wonder how it can be a life of prayer. At other times it can seem such an imperfect offering, a weak vessel, a useless life, so very unlike that phrase in the Anglican Holy Communion liturgy, 'Almighty God, we offer you our souls and bodies, to be a living sacrifice . . .' Of course, this prayer is followed by a request for grace and blessing, but when you are feeling really at the lowest point of your existence, it still seems such a poor thing to offer; or if we do, it is hard to feel strong enough to take on the responsibility.

Being a contemplative can help to give meaning to the crumpled remains of a more active life. If you have always had to rely on others because of a disability it can also help to give a powerful, secret thread in your life.

DEFINING THE WAY

As we grow older, more experienced in the life of prayer, more deeply involved in our inner life; and at the same time, more worldly wise and perhaps, educated; we find it increasingly difficult to describe God. Our definition becomes more hazy and qualified. The Holy Spirit is probably the most difficult part of the Godhead to identify, because we have well established images for the words 'father' and 'son'. Perhaps this difficulty forms part of the veil that will one day be lifted. Perhaps our trusting innocence has become too overlaid by our intellectual reasoning; or we have, in growing closer to God, begun to see something of the complexities of his nature. Whatever the explanation, we know that to attempt to describe him in human terms would be totally inadequate. The new path we are called to follow leads us away from our previous assumptions and the comfortable, familiar surroundings in which we have been content to rest for so long. God often leads us along a path surrounded by mist. It is as if when we round the bend in the path, we just miss seeing him but we know he is ahead. We are also aware that he is beside us, taking our arm to help us over the stones and ditches in our path. Sometimes it seems as if we travel for a long time through featureless country, or the way grows dark and we have to go on believing that the light before us is still there. This is the working out of our personal plan.

Some of us, on the contrary, refuse to begin the journey and arrive at our life's end in the same immature state as we were as infants. One woman I knew some years ago, married and with a family, always said that she found the children's special service the most helpful and it was the one she liked best. This was nothing to do with the content of the service but because it reminded her of her school days and the gentle, comforting experience church had been then. There is nothing wrong in these elements sometimes being present, but in her case she had been prevented from growing in her faith and challenging life with it. Going to the children's service allowed that woman to turn aside from her responsibilities, and her character had changed so that she was selfish, grumbling and unhappy.

Some people arrive at life's end bearing the scars of the journey as joyful medals of the struggle. Some travel steadfastly to the end almost unnoticed by fellow humans but with a quiet satisfaction, or hope, that they really have tried their best and can now accept the rest and peace of death until they are called for the next part of the grand design.

Whatever your condition or situation, the closer you are to God the more possibilities you have to be close to other people, cutting through their outer, often off-putting, appearances; the disreputable tramp is still your brother in God's family. We have all, to some extent, to accept the face people wish to show to us, but a person who spends his life close to God can sometimes reassure others that there is another path if they want to be truly themselves. Your own practice of the presence of God will show itself in the way others can recognise you, when they need to, as a friendly haven. Your abandonment can then be seen as abandonment to the will of God rather than abandonment of the world, and it is possible to be of unexpected service to others.

Begin your new life and continue in it by doing everything for the love of God. The searching for the right way is pleasing to God but we can only find it through the Holy Spirit. If we lost heart and grumble because we 'don't seem to be getting anywhere', we slow down our journey by our discontent. It is not for us to invent progress points, like the check points in a car rally, but rather to journey steadily on and take as wonderful gifts any recognition from God that we seem to be on the right route to him.

6

MAKING SPACE FOR PRAYER

When we are young our prayers are, in a sense, said for us by our parents, teachers, the clergy; it is only when we reach a certain maturity, not necessarily a certain age, that we are able to take on the responsibility ourselves.

Maturity in this area of our lives is a very difficult thing to measure and we must all progress towards it at our own pace. Unlike social skills, it is not very obvious when we have learnt to manage this side of our lives alone, and it is not a part of ourselves that we are usually very anxious to share with anyone. Generally speaking we are reticent about discussing such deeply personal elements of our make-up, and as most of us have very little teaching about prayer, it takes considerable courage to embark on a life of prayer. We can do exercises, follow formulae, but at some point we are required to launch ourselves into the unknown without very much guidance except the inner promptings of God within us.

Getting this part of our lives right means we have less concern for the superfluous things of the world that can so easily engulf us. We gain a different perspective, and because we most probably become far less competitive, we are less concerned with those aspects of apparent success that are generally recognised as signs and symbols of status in worldly terms.

Many of us remember prayers being said with us at bedtime when we were children and we just said 'Amen' or even just listened.

Next came prayers at school in classrooms and assembly time. Here the prayers were often misheard or misunderstood and our responses were often rather garbled. We were not actually taught what to say but picked it up as we went along from our equally mystified neighbours. It was generally assumed that these prayers were an extension of our experience in church, but it was often the case that few children actually went to church. A few were sent, but not many went as a family with their parents.

Perhaps as we got older, school assemblies happened less frequently and were more chaotic when they did. Possibly not much attention was paid when there were rival attractions available and the surrounding atmosphere was one of cynicism. At that age, those who want to join in prayers often have to deal with peer group pressure and ridicule and only the most courageous can cope.

By the time we become adults, most of us have lost the innocent confidence about prayer that we had as children. It has been overlaid with so much else that when we go back to thoughtful, careful praying as adults, we must begin in all simplicity as little children; indeed, few of us are capable of anything else at first.

When we go to church, most of what we need is written down, or said on our behalf if we belong to a non-liturgical tradition. Perhaps horizons can be broadened during the intercessions, but the general pattern is the same: the leader prays and we have a short response. Some people belong to less formal prayer groups, although sometimes these groups develop an intensity which does not suit everyone. And even in this less formal atmosphere the pattern of prayer and response often remains much the same. The crucial point is that whatever we gain from public worship, there is a great gap in our lives if that is our only point of prayer. Some form of private contact with God is also necessary if we are to have a more complete relationship with him.

THE LANGUAGE OF PRAYER

Take a day to listen to other people speaking; at work, on the radio, in the bus etc., and see how references to religion are woven into our everyday speech, including swear words. If you listen carefully you will hear many references, from the jovial to the blasphemous, and yet the speaker probably has no religious intention. So try to be a little more aware of your own speech. If you find yourself using religious expressions as swear words, tidy up your language, reserving those phrases for real prayer. If you need a phrase to use when you would otherwise have sworn, think of a few silly ones for those times when you are deprived of speech by anger or intense irritation – most people swear because they have not got an adequate vocabulary to draw on, on the spur of the moment. By doing this, you are actually creating space in your language, and so in your life, for prayers.

You may enjoy creating family words or picking up something you have read or that particularly applies to your life. Then, when you really do need special help, patience, strength, etc., you can make it a sincere arrow prayer, which will be much more useful. You are already making a start on finding time for prayer.

When you have not had much practice with prayer, it is easy to feel self-conscious when you have to use our own words – even in private – rather than say 'Amen' to someone else's. One of the wonderful things about God is that he never minds how inadequate our prayers seem to us. The very fact that we can approach him, however unpolished our prayers and ragged our thoughts, means that we are opening a door through which he may reach us.

If it helps, to get you started, why not begin with the Lord's Prayer or something else you are familiar with, or feel comfortable about using? At the very beginning you might simply use a prayer you know and then just say, 'Come to my heart, Lord Jesus. There is room in my heart for thee!' Then wait for a minute, thinking over the phrase, before you continue your work. You are beginning to stretch out the time you pray, giving yourself a little longer to think and at the same time, learning to feel more at ease with prayer. The minute you spend at the end, thinking over that short prayer, will help to prepare you for quiet listening.

We have all had the experience of speaking to someone and finding they have not heard us because they have been deep in thought or engrossed in something they were doing. Sometimes there is simply too much noise, as in a busy place like a crowded station platform. With practice you can develop and use this level of concentration for prayer even when you are surrounded by noise and bustle.

RELAXING IN PRAYER

As we have already discovered, the natural rhythm of breathing has, from ancient times, been recognised as something that can be harnessed in our search for God. Try combining a slow, deep inhalation of breath and an even slower one out, with that minute at the end of your prayer – what might be called 'relaxing in God'. With practice, that relaxing in God can be used on its own at times of stress without a set prayer. If it helps, just say in your head, as you breathe out, 'Please help me God', or 'Be with me dear

Lord', or some other very simple prayer.

Try praying as you walk along the street. The pace of steady walking is a good rhythm for prayer and if you can remember a prayer or psalm, it can often fit very neatly into this rhythm. If you cannot remember anything, then make up something very simple. For example: as you breathe in and take, say five steps, 'Praise God for the bright blue sky', and as you breathe out and take five more steps make up a contrasting phrase such as, 'Praise God for the depths of the ocean.' Perhaps something like this would be more suitable at times: 'Be with me, God, as I make this decision', or 'Keep my mind clear from wandering.' With a bit of practice you will soon feel confident in making up suitable sentences.

There are some people who find prayer exercises helpful while others are put off trying by the complicated severity or seeming difficulty of them. That is why I suggest such simple beginnings, in order to help you discover the right way for you.

Because most of us are not very used to sharing very much with God, we often do not think ourselves or our problems important enough to pray about. Sometimes, when we are trying to see things objectively we just forget to pray. I am not suggesting prayer as an alternative method to problem solving, but as an essential additional one.

LIVING IN GOD'S PRESENCE

I have already mentioned Brother Lawrence, and I think that his way of seeing the spiritual dimension of life can be an encouragement to us. He was very much aware of his faults but refused to be discouraged by them. He confessed to God but did not plead to be excused. Lawrence found formal spiritual exercises very difficult, but the personal method he devised for himself took him straight to God.

57

Sometimes through the pressure of work or some other distraction, he forgot about being close to God but when he remembered, he simply said he was sorry for his forget-fulness, thanked God for reminding him and got on with his life again in the presence of God.

Lawrence felt closer to God in his everyday work than when he tried to be quiet somewhere in order to be 'spiritual'. Consulting anyone else about his soul only con-fused him. It is not necessary to have a spiritual director in order to live a life of prayer. Lawrence partly lived by the maxim that instead of doing anything for ourselves, we should do it for God.

From very simple beginnings it is possible to plan out the day so that prayer becomes a part of almost everything we do. The idea of using the pace of our breathing can be practised when we have to do mundane, repetitive jobs, until in time we can begin to look forward to them because we see them as an aid to prayer. In this way formerly non-creative time is turned to gold.

As we grow in our prayer life we are constantly question-ing, doubting and reforming our ideas and understanding. This is not loss of faith, but an active faith that is seeking the closest, most carefully accurate understanding as it applies to each individual one of us. Just as there are times of elation there are also times of shadow and doubt. It is rather like the shadows and reflections of the clouds seen on a hillside; neither the brightness nor the shadow is the whole picture, but the complete weather chart is made up of both these elements. One without the other would be a distortion of the truth. Perhaps, being a contemplative is some part of an expression of our inability to cope alone and a true sense of our own weakness and unworth. Only by having the con-stant prop of prayer for ourselves and by, in some measure, providing that constant prop for others, is life full and as fulfilling as possible. Speaking of the early members of the Church, Thomas à Kempis said 'Every hour seemed short for the service of God and it is possible to be outwardly destitute but inwardly refreshed with grace and divine consolation.'

STRUGGLES IN PRAYER

There is no end to prayer. We can only become better or worse than we were before. Closer or further away from oneness with God. More ready than yesterday but, if all goes well, not as ready as we hope to be next week. Closer or further away from God's intention of what we should be. The constant battle we have with ourselves, rocked by the evil within us, sometimes shows a chink through which we may squeeze a little closer to our best, the best that God has designed for us, that he has put in us, and that we seem so reluctant to accept.

Through our own struggles it is possible to begin to see God in others. We are meant to work with our fellow men and women. To be self-centred and only seeking to be 'good' in a way that ignores our fellow-travellers, is not the way to build heaven. To some extent we have to participate in the struggles of others. To be truly God's human being requires us to have a care for their troubles and triumphs, and to be willing to accept from them comfort, care and guidance as well as having our own viewpoints accepted and our gifts valued. If we could retire to an island and work out our own path to God, it might be easy, we think, but it can never be true because the human family is what we are all part of, and it is with that family that God wants us to succeed.

It is when we all get together that so much trouble starts. The sum of our individual evil can become a power that is

59

hardly controllable. Our weaknesses challenge and react to real or imaginary challenges and criticisms. Our less well-developed boldness for good becomes swamped, and it is often difficult to call a halt to the destructive powers of the worst parts of us.

Generally speaking, anything that involves effort in overcoming difficulties, either physical or mental, brings with it a greater reward than the easy things. So I am not suggesting that you pray only when it is easy, or when you are in distress, but I do suggest that you take on an added burden of something that you can acknowledge to be difficult. We all have areas of life which we find hard; it may be certain relationships, or ideas, or the ideals of others. So why not earmark one or two of these to be worked on? This means that you bring to a subject your intellect and your willingness to explore, and your prayer, at times other than when you have actually to confront the problem, and away from the emotions it might rouse in the heat of the moment. By taking on such an exercise you give yourself time to bring your whole personality to deal with it, rather than just your irritated emotions. You are positively including God in your deliberations.

Our willingness to attempt the life of prayer is constantly challenged by the 'humanness' within us. Often our trust in God is not wholehearted because we do not feel certain that God hears us. But whether or not we feel able to pray, God is already active in our lives, and part of our contribution to his work is the positive acceptance and acknowledgement of this; showing that we are ready to co-operate in an expression of our love and trust. God is the source and the final destination of our prayer.

However hard prayer may be, the rewards are out of all proportion to the effort. We are liable to be deceived by the excuses we make for ourselves for not making the effort.

60

The reasons we give ourselves to excuse our failure are the most miserable and weak parts of our human personality. These parts can so easily distort our outer lives that we need to be very firm with ourselves if they are not to attack and warp our inner life also.

Prayer is intangible. The contemplative is called to spend energy on something that cannot be measured like essays being written, or digging the garden, or teaching something that will help other people to pass exams. Whatever other calls are made on your time by 'worldly' work and responsibilities, a great deal of waking time is to be expended on this intangible exercise. It may not seem justifiable to other people because it is essentially a one-to-one experience with God, but if you feel that God is really calling you to this sort of relationship then you will be able to work out a way of weaving this part of your life into the more mundane expressions of your existence.

WHAT CAN YOUR PRAYER DO?

It is possible that by your repeated care through prayer, someone will receive relief from pain or distress or find the strength to face a hard life or a difficult event. God always listens to our prayers, but we do not always understand his response.

Why should you be chosen for this special sort of prayer life? Perhaps your special combination of qualities and reserves of strength, and your insight, are exactly right for the particular work you are being prepared for. We are all so different – and perhaps this is a simple illustration of one of the reasons for our diversity. There are endless patterns of support possible for us all, in whatever biological, genetic, environmental ways this support is brought about. From the God-given basics, physical and spiritual, our lives go on to be shaped by circumstances and the people we meet. God is perfectly able to match people creatively in ways which may seem to us strange and inappropriate.

It is difficult to answer another's questions about your particular relationship with God except in very general terms, or by comparing it with what seems to be something rather similar in their own experience. Being closer to God does not mean that there will be more times when the answers to your prayers will be obviously positive. You must still be prepared for the answer to be 'no'. And if you try to force the direction, God will most probably still say 'no'; you must be open for the new way he is suggesting.

SO WHAT NEXT?

Try to establish a pattern of prayer with the subjects that are given to you in periods of quiet listening. There will always be times when you are suddenly moved to pray for someone or something, but this is in addition to your regular pattern. Some help with finding your pattern is given in the next chapter.

Try to be open enough to take on topics that are difficult. Most of us have experienced the quiet relief and joy that comes when we have worked through a difficult relationship with someone, even if we are also feeling rather bruised and battered by the experience. Something rather similar can occur in prayer. Plan the day round whatever 'markers' are right for you. Do not be too ambitious to start with or you may soon leave off.

Try to vary your programme so that it includes such aspects as prayer, meditation, reading, quiet listening, asking for guidance.

Perhaps find a different person to pray for every day; someone you know, or have only seen in the street, or heard or read about. There are always many who need your prayers or who would benefit from some extra prayer.

Pray for yourself, too. This will come in waves and there will be more or less to pray about, according to circumstances. There will be times of great intensity and many times of doubt and barrenness. It may seem that God is really pushing you beyond what you feel capable of. But if he gives you something very hard, he will also give support and help, sometimes from unexpected quarters. Always be receptive and flexible enough for the unexpected.

When you have had time to think about the change that will be made in your day to day living if you follow a contemplative way of life, you may decide to refuse God's calling. He may need to ask you many times; it could take years for you to interpret your call in the appropriate way. You will possibly send yourself, or be misled, down other paths; but you can be sure that God will not give up. If this is the right way for you it will become so clear that any other alternative would be absurd.

Remember that the longest journey starts with one step.

7

MAKING A START

Simply by making a beginning on a more prayerful way of
life you make yourself available to the possibility of more of
God's mystery and love being revealed to you. You must be
patient, however. It is possible to live a life of careful
endeavour and perhaps to achieve a great deal spiritually,
but to feel at the end of such a life that not much has been
accomplished. It is really not up to us to make the final
measurement but simply to follow the signposts and go
through the doors God shows us. We are not competing
with anyone, but making our own progress in the place God
has put us and the conditions he has given us to cope with.

Ways to God are probably as many and as different as
there are people. Some ways seem stony and hard, devoid of
softening and comforting help, while others seem surrounded by reassurances and encouragements.

God, who created all the wonders about us, both visible
and invisible, can also call closer those for whom church
allegiance is difficult or impossible. We may not judge or be
dismissive of other people's ways, but only say that one way
rather than another seems right for us.

God is the foundation of our prayer and it is his will that
we should pray. In time he can make it our will too, and he
can encourage us to pray inwardly even when we do not
enjoy it. Prayer that comes from illness or emptiness or a
feeling of barrenness in prayer, is even more pleasing to

God because he wants us to be responsible enough to work away at our prayers in all circumstances.

I have said that my own call to the contemplative life came out of severe illness. Some of what follows, then, comes from my own experience, and may not apply directly to your own life. But I hope it will show how even the most unpromising circumstances can provide a basis for developing an active prayer life.

STARTING FROM SUFFERING

In suffering we share in the sadness and distress of God and at some level share in the reality of Christ as the 'suffering servant'. Making a start on a new life at a time when the odds seem so much against us requires enormous effort, but the experience can be a true point of growth. Sometimes it is good to know pain and wretchedness in order that we may have some small inkling of how good and gracious and sustaining God can be.

An amount of suffering can be useful in life, not because it makes us nobler or better, but because it helps us to appreciate the goodness of more normal times and to have an understanding of the trials of others. Through suffering we can become more loving. It can even be argued that sometimes the suffering of someone who is close to God is greater because he has a greater awareness of human potential for good and sees, perhaps more clearly, how selfishness and greed, made manifest in the hurting of others, is destructive of those who practise it when it could, instead, be converted into positive energies.

It has been suggested that those who suffer very greatly are particularly close to God. Mother Julian said that suffering can be seen as a purging after which we might be closer to God. Brother Lawrence thought that God often sends diseases of the body to cure those of the soul. I suggest, therefore, that if you are called to suffering, you pray not for relief, but for strength to endure the suffering. Those who practise healing through the laying on of hands claim that there is always comfort, sometimes relief and very rarely, a cure. Prayers from suffering, about suffering, could be said to follow the same pattern.

Prayer can transform restricted surroundings from a prison to a haven. If illness or infirmity forces you to withdraw, do not be angry but rather learn to be thankful that you have had certain difficulties and challenges and distractions removed from you in order that you may concentrate on things of the spirit.

MAKING GOOD USE OF PAIN

Even such a seemingly useless thing as constant pain can be put to good use with time and determination. If you try to relax about the whole idea of living with pain, it is possible to analyse it so that you can use it as a reminder to pray. We must assume that whatever medical advice necessary has been taken and that you are facing pain as a way of life, perhaps for the rest of your life. I will discuss prayer plans later, but if the pain is the same recurring, one, you can use it as a reminder to you to pray, or to continue with the prayer plan you have worked out for your day.

If the pain, or different pains, are felt in different parts of your body, it can be useful to make out a 'body prayer map'. Designate different concerns to different parts of your body, and when you feel pain in that particular place you are reminded to pray for the people, place or concern that you have designated to that spot. If the pain fluctuates in intensity, increase your concentration on prayer with the increase of the pain. It may well be that you can perfect this

66

method to such a degree that you no longer have so much pain because you are more attuned to its significance as a pointer to prayer; so that when the pain is first felt you have a well-rehearsed routine that carries you beyond the reach of physical discomfort. With practice you can learn how to pace your praying to correspond with the time of the pain. You may eventually even learn to welcome pain because of the depths of your prayer life and the closeness with God that it heralds. If you are very fortunate, some pain can become more of a 'sensation' rather than something hurtful.

Another useful sort of prayer map is to use the plan of your home as a guide to prayer. If, for example, it takes you a long time to go upstairs, make a sequence of prayers for the stairs. It is up to you which subjects you choose, but it means that if you have to pause on each step, that pause can be put to positive use by praying rather than just to groan. Each step can have attached to it a different person or idea or event; or it could be a series of prayers such as thanksgiving or praise, with the Gloria kept for the top step!

With a bit of thought the whole house can be divided in this fashion so that your progress round the building, whether you are living with pain or not, can be a progress of prayer. It is possible to carry this idea further into the daily round, and it is up to the individual as to how far this is helpful.

I suggest that you try the 'prayer maps' and the breathing exercises that follow, on a small scale to start with and see how they suit you. After all, you have nothing to lose and possibly a great deal to gain. St John of the Ladder, in the seventh century, said, 'Let the memory of Jesus combine with your breath and then you will know the profit of silence.'

BREATHING AND DEEP BREATHING

We have all, within our daily lives, the machinery to help us cope with stress and challenge. We sometimes hear people say, 'So I took a deep breath and went into the manager's office'; or, 'I had to count to ten before I spoke.' The extended use of the natural process of breathing can bring wonderful benefits, both physical and mental.

We have already looked (in chapter 4) at a simple way of combining breathing with prayer. Here are some more advanced exercises which you may find helpful.

Most of us use only the top few inches of our lungs and miss the chance of putting to use their full capacity. Our organs need the oxygen carried in the bloodstream from the lungs to function properly, and if they are starved of this essential item, they become sluggish and often illness follows. Most of us need practice and exercises to extend our lung power and thus bring benefit to the whole body. The cleansing processes are speeded up and our bodies have a better chance of functioning well if we first get our lungs working properly.

Because many of us lead such busy lives I am going to suggest some exercises that can be fitted into a normal day. Do not be over-ambitious, because you are probably correcting a fault that you have established over many years. The aim is to increase lung capacity and control. Later you will see how it can be fitted into a prayer routine.

If you have the opportunity, you can do the exercises while you are waiting for the kettle to boil, or sitting quietly somewhere, or at some other moment when nothing very much is happening. Alternatively you might fit them in while you walk to the bus to work; in fact, as I have already said, a steady walking pace can be the ideal rhythm for breathing exercises. It often helps to find a particular job or time of day suitable to the individual, so that we are reminded to do the exercise when that time or regular job occurs.

Exercise 1

First of all, just breathe normally, gently and steadily, so that you establish a rhythm that makes you aware of your breathing: breathe in for a steady count of four and out for a count of four. That could be four steps breathing in and four steps breathing out. When you have established this, make the count longer – five, seven, ten. There must be no strain, and this must be done over a number of days or weeks as your capacity gradually increases. After a few days you should find yourself stepping out more briskly and generally feeling a lot livelier. Even if you are not able to go for a walk, you will most likely experience a feeling of brightness and be more alert.

Exercise 2

Breathe in for a count of five, hold your breath for a count of five and breathe out for a count of five. You should still have some breath left to breathe out with as you reach five. Count silently in your head so that the breath is not used up with speech. When you feel comfortable with this, move on to a count of seven, ten, fifteen, etc. You should always have some breath left for when you reach the number you are aiming at. This is not meant to be rigorous, so take the whole thing slowly and take as many days or weeks as you need. It is a bit like slimming; you have taken a long time to put on the weight, or in this case to cultivate bad habits of breathing, so you must not expect to correct it all in the first week. It may take many weeks to reach twenty; we all vary in our capacity and dedication.

Exercise 3A

By now you will have begun to expand your lungs and they will be getting used to having a proper job to do. Take a normal breath and breathe out. Next take another steady, deeper breath, and breathe out. Then take a really deep breath and breathe out slowly, counting in your head. The first time you will probably be disappointed with your performance, but go on trying. If you work at it and build up performance gradually, you may eventually reach fifty or sixty, but it is essential to advance steadily.

Exercise 3B

This time take the three deep breaths as described above, but when you breathe out on the third, control the breath and make the soft hissing sound: 'ssssss'. Gradually build up the length of the hissing time, always just using enough breath to make the slightest audible sound. Do not push out the sound, but let it come very gently, without effort.

NOW YOU ARE READY TO USE THESE EXERCISES IN PRAYER

Most of us from time to time hear some words in church that stick in our mind. Even if you are not able to go to church, there are other sources. I suggest that for the moment you think of a phrase or sentence that is fairly musical, or at least that can be said with a musical sense without distortion. Combining controlled breathing with praying is a very ancient tradition in many cultures and for me it seems an ideal way of getting extra time out of a normal event. I have found that a count of six is a good rate of steady thoughtful breathing for me, and something about this length can be used without strain by most people. Here are a few suggestions of phrases to get you started. Use them with alternate breaths in and out.

70

Lord have mercy upon us. Christ have mercy upon us.
Help my life to be a living sacrifice. O Lord Jesus, hide
me under the shadow of thy wing.

Just repeat the joined phrases as many times as you find
helpful.

For walking along try: Praise the Lord, praise the Lord;
may the Lord's name be praised.

The *Magnificat* from the Anglican form of Evening Prayer
is easy to learn and remember. It is just the right length and
seems to me very suitable for a breathing prayer, and is good
for walking or cleaning the windows or any other chore that
does not require your whole attention.

> My soul proclaims the greatness of the Lord:
>> my spirit rejoices in God my saviour;
> for he has looked with favour on his lowly servant:
>> from this day all generations will call me
>> blessèd;
> the Almighty has done great things for me:
>> and holy is his name.
> He has mercy on those who fear him:
>> in every generation.
> He has shown the strength of his arm:
>> he has scattered the proud in their conceit.
> He has cast down the mighty from their thrones:
>> and has lifted up the lowly.
> He has filled the hungry with good things:
>> and the rich he has sent away empty.
> He has come to the help of his servant Israel:
>> for he has remembered his promise of mercy,
> the promise he made to our fathers:
>> to Abraham and his children for ever.
> Glory to the Father and to the Son:
>> and to the Holy Spirit;

as it was in the beginning is now:
and shall be for ever. Amen.

Also the *Gloria in excelsis* from Morning Prayer.

Glory to God in the highest:
and peace to his people on earth.
Lord God heavenly King:
almighty God and Father,
we worship you we give you thanks:
we praise you for your glory.
Lord Jesus Christ only Son of the Father:
Lord God Lamb of God,
you take away the sin of the world:
have mercy on us;
you are seated at the right hand of the Father:
receive our prayer.
For you alone are the Holy One:
you alone are the Lord,
you alone are the Most High
Jesus Christ with the Holy Spirit:
in the glory of God the Father. Amen.

Repeating the same phrases over and over can sometimes help you to see new meaning in them, or give them new emphasis, or open up your imagination to a new application. You will be surprised at how your mind sets to work on a new idea from this simple triggering device.

Do not disregard 'secular' phrases that can be used prayerfully, or phrases that spring out of your own experience and which say, in your own words, something valuable. Make a small collection either in a notebook or just in your head, of suitable phrases or ideas that can be used in this way. A suggestion would be to have a few phrases in several different sections. For example, there may be a pressing need that has to be prayed for or a particularly difficult day that has to be focused on. Or you may choose a particular type of concern outside your own life that can be prayed for in this way. Remember too, one or two broader areas such as the overseas work of the church, or the world's children, or politicians, or whatever you feel a natural affinity with.

From the general, move on to the particular. Perhaps someone you know needs extra support just now. Whatever you decide, choose one or two phrases for each type that you can use during the day at odd moments. Tomorrow could be different or the same, depending on events. When you have trained yourself to do this, it will become second nature to you and you will find that in all your odd moments you will automatically tune in to a prayer.

Eventually it may become a prayer without words. This can best be described as a surge of energy or prayer-laden electricity directed to the subject of your choice. It is a sort of sending of the holy cavalry, but instead of soldiers you are sending back-up prayers, supportive thoughts and generally being a channel for whatever God sees as the present need. But all this may come only years after your initial training. For the moment keep it short, simple and relaxed.

RELAX AND GROW BEAUTIFUL

To be able to function adequately most of us need to remain alert during the working day. This does not, however, mean that we cannot also be relaxed, for by the word 'relaxation' I am not referring to the switching off of our sensor terminals, but what in fact amounts to a greater sensitivity because our bodies are enabled to function more completely.

Next time you sit down, just check over your body and see how relaxed you are physically. Are your fists tightly clenched or is your jaw rigid? Are you really resting your legs or sitting stiffly? Are your shoulders hunched or are you making the best use of the chair for a rest? When you go to bed tonight, check that you are really resting your head on the pillow and not holding your neck stiffly. A good way of beginning to learn to relax is by doing it in bed. When you first get into bed take two steady breaths and then make sure that the next breath is slowly breathed in and very slowly breathed out. As you breathe slowly out, try to imagine you are gently sinking through the bed and let all your muscles go with that sinking feeling.

So many of us waste valuable energy and praying time on frowning when we could show a pleasanter face to the world. 'Relax and grow beautiful' may sound glib, but the results will show outwardly and you will feel calmer and more able to cope with the day.

Another simple way to approach relaxation is by getting in touch with the muscles that most often tend to be tensed. Here are a few more simple exercises for you to try. If you are unable to retreat for a special time on your own, try to fit them into some time when you are not concerned with other people – such as when you are in the bath or combing your hair. This is not complicated if you take it step by step.

Exercise 4

Screw up your face as tightly as you can and then relax. Do this twice and then at the third time, as you relax, let your head come forward so that you can feel the skin on your face almost separating from the bones. Now you will start to be aware of the dozens of muscles in the face.

Exercise 5

Take a deep breath and screw up your face and then relax as you breathe out. This time keep your head up as you breathe out and imagine your face becoming very smooth.

Exercise 6

Help to relax your jaw by stretching your mouth from a tight 'oo' shape to a very broad smile.

Exercise 7

Stand with your back straight and your weight a little more on the front of your feet than your heels. It is possible to stand for longer periods like this. Be as balanced as possible and think of your head being exactly in the middle of your shoulders. Imagine it is a ball delicately balanced on a stalk. Many people get into poor posture habits which make them tire easily. Face the front with the middle of your nose lining up with the space between your big toes. The line you could draw between your ears should be level and be parallel with your waist when your hips are level.

You can do this exercise in a chair too, just by moving slightly and keeping your back as straight as possible and by allowing your hands to rest in your lap. Do not fold your hands together but let them rest on your legs with the palms uppermost or facing down, whichever is the most natural and comfortable for you.

We are all guilty from time to time of tensing our neck and shoulders and suffering in consequence. When you feel balanced, let your head roll forward until you feel a slight pulling sensation at the back of your neck. Now let your head roll gently from side to side. It may help you to relax if you have a mental picture of a barrel rolling backwards and forwards, or a tree branch waving in the wind. Do this four or five times and then, with your head still down, hunch your shoulders up and down and let your arms flop loosely like a rag doll's. If you are doing this exercise in a chair, just allow your arms to move as freely as possibly in your lap.

When you have hunched your shoulders four or five times, raise your head into that well balanced stalk position, relax your shoulders and stretch your neck upwards. Take a good breath and breathe out as you stretch up your neck. Imagine that soothing feeling going over you from the top of your head, over your shoulders, down your arms to emerge through your fingertips.

With practice you will be able to relax your face, neck and shoulders without the preliminary exercises, just by taking a deep breath, putting up your head and allowing a flowing feeling of relaxation to wash over your face, over your shoulders and through your fingertips. This ability will help you to stay calmer, give others something pleasanter to look at and save your muscles from getting tight and aching. You can do this brief form of exercise anywhere: waiting for a bus, standing at the checkout, sunbathing, watching television, listening to Grandma telling of her finest hour for the nth time.

When you feel comfortable with this, try combining with it the prayer phrases you have memorised, or even just let some natural happy feeling about the day be verbalised, for instance, 'Thank you, God, for the lovely warm sunshine.' 'Thank you, God, that my friend seems better today.' 'Thank you, God, for helping me cope with that difficult problem.' Even when the day seems totally full of frustration, problems and disaster, it is usually possible to find some small thing to be thankful for.

You can, of course, combine the deep breathing/ relaxation sensation with a prayer asking for help. Perhaps you have a difficult meeting to attend. Before you go in, take a deep breath and as you breathe out and remember to relax, just say, quite simply: 'Please help me, God; you know how nervous I am. Please help me, God, to understand this difficulty/to give of my best/to be guided by you', or any other line that seems appropriate.

The whole idea of this approach to a life of prayer is that it is a relaxed, simple, sincere, continuous event into which you can put more or less effort depending on the requirements of your surrounding life in the world. When you are finding it difficult to understand something, just say, 'Please God, help my understanding', and offer the problem to him. You will be pleased by how the day can be helped along by 'tuning into base' from time to time.

Do not expect a cartoon thunderbolt and a pointing finger. God has given us a certain capacity for understanding, and talents to be used, and he expects us to use them fully. Sometimes after a prayer, the answers become very clear, as we say 'like someone switching on a light'. But most of the time, thinking prayerfully does not produce spectacular results but it helps you to feel supported, and encouraged to use your God-given faculties to the full.

SELF DENIAL

Each day is a new chance to begin again. We know that through our repentance and God's forgiveness we are constantly being given fresh chances and we have to try to be as generous in receiving them as God is in giving them. God wants us to accept the true absolution that is so lovingly given, and to appreciate that tomorrow really is a new opportunity for good. If we always try to do the best we can, our small failings will not seem so destructive.

Sometimes we feel like punishing ourselves for the times when we feel we have not lived up to the ideals we have set for ourselves, but I do not wish to discuss that here except to mention something that might appear, to the outsider, to be the same thing. Denying oneself comforts, treats or happy occasions can so easily be mistaken by others for disapproval. They misinterpret your path to God through self denial, and see you as a spoil sport or condemning their frivolity. It is hard for others, not similarly engaged, to understand why you deny yourself innocent pleasures for something you may hope to gain later and for which they can see very little evidence. Because of that possibility of misunderstanding, if for no other reason, it is best to keep your prayer life as private as possible.

If the Holy Spirit is calling you to this kind of life you can, at best, only prepare yourself to be receptive to what God will do next. All our exercises, physical and mental, can only get us into training for something else and are not an end in themselves. Whatever way you choose to be closer to God, it should become so much part of you that eventually it becomes second nature. This practice initiates the two-way process; so that your prayers are offered to and you may receive succour from God.

Do not be impatient, for it may take a long time to reach the goal you have set yourself or the notion *you* have of perfection or holiness – which may not be God's! We have, rather, to be content with God's pace, whether it is very slow or startlingly fast.

REGULAR PRAYING

Apart from whatever constant prayer you manage to weave into your everyday life, you have to face the fact that it is not always easily sustainable. Therefore, special regular prayer times are to be encouraged, although we may not always feel like bothering, or may feel we have nothing to say. Do not forget that God is waiting for you to put aside the absorbing things of everyday life in order to speak to you in quiet. Try to find a time to put aside other distractions and just wait quietly and calmly. There may not be any noticeable 'result', but each time you are further preparing yourself and showing yourself more willing for God's coming.

Morning and evening are good times to pray. The morning can help you to set your plan for the day and to pray about some of the things you know you will encounter. In the evening you can look back over the day and see how it has worked, and from your findings perhaps make resolutions for the next day, pray for forgiveness for your blindness to the needs of others, say sorry for your careless and unkind actions and pray for a better day tomorrow. It sometimes helps always to say your daily prayers in the same place; even if you live in one room you can literally turn your back on the distractions of your world simply by turning a chair to the wall.

This sort of physical act can be a great help, especially if you can arrange to do it at the same time every day. Try to get into a good habit of daily prayer, even if it will only, at first, work for you by giving you a guilty conscience when the planned time comes round. When you manage to follow the plan you will see after a few minutes how restorative prayer can be. I have found it helpful to have a few set prayers that I always say, when I am able to, at my special morning and evening prayer times. Although, if you choose to follow this pattern, these will be genuine prayers, they will also serve the purpose of helping you to be quiet and getting in the mood for prayer.

Whether in public or private devotions, it is often quite useful actually to read some of the very familiar prayers you have perhaps been using for many years. You may well be surprised by what you have been taking for granted or overlooking for such a long time. You may even discover that a particular prayer will have special meaning for you, or can be used in a way you had not thought of before. Sometimes you will just want to be quiet after you have said your introduction to your prayers. Consider using a suitable phrase instead of, or as well as, prayer. The few minutes, or just a short pause, after this is a way of giving space to God. After a few minutes, say the closing prayer and go back to your normal life.

PLANNING YOUR DAY

Examine the day and teach yourself discipline so that you can make full use of it. It is said that you should always ask a busy person to do a job for you because he is disciplined and will find a way to fit in something extra; but someone who has all day to do a job will probably take all day to do it. An artist cannot afford to sit around waiting for inspiration but must work steadily day after day, and if inspiration comes as well, that is a bonus.

In rethinking and organising your day, plan where you can steal extra time. There are a few minutes of every day when most of us have time alone; but getting away for what seems like self-indulgent peace and quiet in order to pray or meditate requires determination, so lengthen any time you do have alone by two minutes each time. Two minutes can be quite a long time to use at the outset. Two minutes multiplied by ten times a day soon begins to be a useful amount of time. Try to sit quietly and do this while you are waiting for the bath to fill; or combine it with cleaning your teeth, going upstairs or hanging out the washing.

If you feel these are not suitable times because they are too mixed up with ordinary things, you must consider whether these stolen moments are really the only time you have. You may come to two conclusions: a) that this really is the only time you have, and it is better to do this than not to pray at all – and in any case it feels good to weave God closer into the fabric of everyday life; or b) that if you get better organised you really can squeeze a few minutes of quiet out of the busy day. It all goes back to the question of being efficient. Pray as you begin a particularly irksome job, and pray during a boring one. Remember also that to do something really well for God's sake, is a form of prayer.

Choose a concern that you can feel deeply about or which has some special link with your own life and invent a few short, prayerful sentences about it, that you can easily remember. It does not matter how simple they are. Choose one of these to think about in spare moments during the day, such as when you are taking in the milk bottles, or walking to the front door to collect the letters. You will soon learn to enjoy these extra opportunities for prayer.

PLANNING YOUR WEEK

Plan the week in a similar way to how you plan the day. You can, of course, include more concerns, but do not be over-ambitious. Make a realistic plan that you really feel there is some possibility of keeping to. You must guard against being so immersed in your own world of prayer that you neglect your duties as a member of the community.

In planning your week it will help to have some variety in the types of prayer you use. Times for intercession need to be mixed with praise and thanksgiving, a quiet time for receiving and welcoming requests from God and for simply 'tuning in to headquarters' for your own refreshment. As with planning a day, a few repeating prayers and phrases can be useful. Use any prayers, phrases, poems, verses and ideas that you have jotted down in your notebook as the basis for meditation. A few well-thought out arrow prayers are useful to have ready for when you need them. As you get really interested in prayers and praying, you will, perhaps, want to prepare special prayers to use when you are depressed or particularly worried. The Anglican *Alternative Service Book* has special prayers for public use, but we need them too in our personal armoury. I have already mentioned some of the 'input' for your prayer plans, but you may also find it helpful to try to remember something to which our prayers could be attached for the week. It is possible, if you go to church, that something in the sermon will seem particularly relevant, and that could be the outline of your plan that week.

Other input sources, or outposts for refreshment, can be discovered through reading the Bible and other Christian literature. It is generally more useful if you can follow a regular Bible reading plan, rather than just dipping into it. Most churches can provide a plan of readings that will take you right through the Bible in two years but have a short enough passage each day so that it is possible to reflect on what you have read. There are also many Bible reading notes available such as those published by the Bible Reading Fellowship, the Scripture Union, and the International Bible Reading Association.

A browse round a religious bookshop will produce much that is interesting to read, and there are a number of Christian newspapers and magazines with a wide variety of articles to set you thinking in a new and exciting way.

Sometimes there are pamphlets at the back of a church, or posters. Something like this could well set you off on a useful train of thought if you are open and aware enough to make use of it. Hymns and psalms can also catch the imagination with a subject for meditation. The danger is that you will be overwhelmed by all the possibilities once you really make a start, and it becomes a bit like regretting that it is impossible to read all the books in the world; so you have to be very selective and just make good use of a few.

There are many non-religious sources too, especially these days when media coverage is so good and deals with so many subjects in an easily digestible form. A daily newspaper will provide endless topics for prayer.

PLANNING AHEAD

When you are able to work out a plan for a week, you can go on to make an outline plan for a month. And as the year progresses your planning can be helped by the way the Christian year is observed in the churches, with the different festivals and seasons. Advent and Lent are two seasons that are already precisely worked out for anyone who is a regular churchgoer but even if you are not, it can be helpful to plan a number of weeks together so that you can see the end of a particular endeavour and have a goal to work towards. There is always something to be said for anything that encourages perseverance. The church festivals are useful markers, and they can help to break up the year into manageable portions.

Human beings sometimes like to make grand gestures and grand plans, but because we are only human it helps if, instead of saying you are changing your life for the rest of your life, you can invent short-term goals for yourself that have very practical boundaries.

I have mentioned only a few ways to bring variety into your prayer life and I am confident you can think of many more. Later on, when you are less self-conscious about praying and have had more experience in fitting this sort of prayer into an ordinary busy life, you should consider keeping a prayer diary in which you jot down brief notes on what you plan to pray about, and what you have prayed. Sometimes the intention and what you actually do pray about can be very far apart. Perhaps, when you read the diary through later you will be able to see a progression from chaos to order, as you learn prayer discipline and settle to a form that suits your life and personality.

8

SUITING THE STYLE TO THE SITUATION

In this busy and competitive world, our immediate daily concerns – going to work, running a home, being responsible for a family, wanting to spend time with them and have some free time for ourselves – can fill the horizon and you may well feel it would be impossible to take on anything else. What I am suggesting is that just as we spring clean our homes or desks every so often, we should also consider doing the same with our lives and minds.

Take a long, hard look at your lifestyle. Of what is the day composed? Are you juggling work outside the home with heavy commitments within the home? Are you at home all day but never seem to get time to do so many of the things you plan or would like to be able to find time for? Whatever basics you start with you can probably be more efficient. 'Efficient' is one of those words that has a rather stark, businesslike ring to it but I do not mean that your life should be run like a factory, just that you should have the feeling at the end of the day, that you are realising much more of your full potential as a person.

Why not try a simple time and motion study of your life? Begin by sorting out what you really consider it necessary to do in your given circumstances. Can some jobs be avoided altogether? If you don't polish all the furniture every week the heavens will not fall, and that will leave you a bit of extra time. It may be possible to combine some jobs or cut out some of the stages. A mundane example from my own life is cooking scrambled eggs. For years I mixed the eggs in a separate bowl while the knob of butter melted in the pan, but now I just put everything into the pan together and the eggs taste exactly the same, some washing up is saved and I like to believe that I have an extra bit of time for something else that seems more important.

When you think about it, you can probably find lots of jobs in your life that could either be combined or discarded altogether without making you feel guilty, or driving you to change your diet to prepackaged junk food. Never making an empty-handed journey does not mean that you will always be thinking about work but that you are getting more efficient at making time for things you really want to do.

Wherever you are, draw up a list of the jobs you must do every day, week, month. Do these jobs follow Parkinson's Law and expand to fill the time available? Try to make a new, realistic, plan for a few of your days, and include some time for leisure activities. Make some time to be quiet, if only for a few minutes. As I suggested earlier, a few extra minutes in the bath or some such other time, can be just what you need to keep your life in perspective.

Stop worrying about things you cannot control, or the future which you cannot shape. If you are really worried and there is some possibility of your action being effective, then go out and act. Otherwise stop wasting mental time and energy on it. Stop being nosy! A proper care and concern for others is good, but a nosy busybody is no one's friend. So clear your mind of that sort of inquisitiveness and you will have more time for something more positive.

It can very often be helpful to set a deadline by which you must make a decision. Difficult issues do take more time and it is right and proper to use time to get a better perspective on a big decision; time for the immediate anger, anxiety or shock to fade away a little before you are in a reasonable and stable enough state of mind to make a major rational decision. But there are many items cluttering up our heads that really could be better dealt with on a more realistic time scale; for example, choosing new curtains or a new dress or where to go on holiday. To be more efficient, make a deadline and keep to it and after you have made the decision *stop thinking about the problem*. Even the most hardworking or overworked of us can sometimes be guilty of frittering away our thinking time on trivialities. It is possible to organise our mental, thinking, time as effectively as our physical, working, time. If we are able and have the discipline to concentrate, when we are really required to, on what we are doing, the remaining time can be stretched and expanded into useful thinking or praying time.

One sort of life does not exclude another, parallel, spiritual one, but you must not skimp the physical job for the prayer life. Part of being complete is doing your job, whether inside the home or out, to the best of your ability. To have said of you 'His mind is always somewhere else', or, 'She never seems to have her mind on the job', is not complimentary. We are all, on occasions, distracted by anxieties, and that is understandable, but God's plan will not be served if the balance of your life becomes warped. Praying outwards from your own situation helps you to pray and not to allow your own concerns to block your view of other people's problems. And in the process you feel better, too.

Try to find a few minutes at the beginning of the day to commit yourself and the day to God. In time you will soon discover a few minutes extra during which you may perhaps enjoy silently singing a hymn or a modern Christian song. Even if you do not know all the words, the tune can be part of your worship.

Instead of getting irritated by small things, begin to use some of the time created by your increased efficiency for thinking more deeply about the irritation, and ask God's help to deal with it. In time you will probably develop a variety of short prayers that you can repeat when you expect interruptions, so that you will not need to experience frustration when the immediate needs of the physical world seem to impinge on your prayer life. Make yourself learn the deep breathing and relaxation exercises so that when you do find time to sit down, you really can relax and so make the best possible use of a moment or two of rest.

The sort of prayer life that becomes almost a running commentary on your day can be very tiring, so plan when you are going to take some time off and you will return to your prayer pattern with renewed determination and pleasure.

STAYING AT HOME TO WORK

The number of women who juggle outside work with running a home increases every year, but there are also many men who want to play a fuller part in family life and they too have to find the time and the energy to fulfil their ideal of a good parent or spouse. Many and varied are the sociological reasons why the home is becoming increasingly important in the lives of people in our society.

There are a great many people whose main area of functioning is the home, and if I list just a few of them you will see how varied they are. The mother with young children; anyone with old or ill relatives who need constant care; the retired who are not very old; those who are old or ill or both. Those who do not need to work but put their time at home to use for others. Those whose lives are bound up with the work of their spouses. The unemployed; the person who works from home; the part-time worker. If you stay at home from choice, a regime of prayer can make this way of life even better. If you do not want to be at home, a regime of prayer can make it bearable and perhaps an eventual joy.

If you have to stay at home it is easy to feel rejected and only half alive. If you take on a life of prayer it will be as if, when others go out to work, you go inwards. There is a great feeling of satisfaction to be had, which is not false pride, but a feeling of being useful, if your prayer life is strong, instead of feeling you are just dragging out the days with Grandma or whatever most of your time is taken up with.

From early Christian times there has been a strong tradition of prayer in the remote western highlands and islands of Scotland. It is part of the Gaelic tradition that there are prayers for every possible domestic occasion. Not just festival times, but each mundane job has its own prayer and there are many involving the elements and the environment too, by which, of course, so many more lives were governed in earlier times. Seeing the power and energy of the elements as manifestations of the power of God, christianised what had before been terrifying. The harsh northern weather became acceptable and glorious when God was recognised through it.

A good starting point for combining prayer with everyday life could be to pick out something in your life that you feel strongly about, or that always irritates you, and start to think prayerfully about it.

Many years ago we were visited regularly by a gentleman of the roads. His visits were not close together and in between we entertained many rogues on the doorstep, but for some reason this particular man always irritated me. Thinking about it, I came to realise that the cup of tea or the meal I gave him could just as easily be given with a pleasant friendly face as with an unfriendly one. Having prepared myself, I was able, when he next called, to say a quick arrow prayer to firm my resolve, and from then on I was no longer irritated by him and that wasted energy of anger was rechannelled to better use.

When we care for children we usually have the reward of seeing them grow and develop. Even with the mentally retarded there is usually hope, even if it is unfounded, that there will be an eventual breakthrough. Looking after old people, when even those you love can be irritating, can often be the worst sort of caring, for invariably there is only deterioration and they often change into what seems little more than a lingering shadow of the lively person they used to be.

The old and the ill frequently have a deep sense of shame, while they are still able to feel anything, in their incapacity to cope, and this makes them difficult to look after in a way that does not offend them. They need to be given time, and the carer has often to listen to many repeated stories and questions. It is as if the old people need to affirm their existence by hearing someone speak to them. If you are in this situation of staying at home to care for someone, train yourself to endure all the repeats by praying for the person. This constant 'low level' praying can be continued through sitting with, nursing, playing with and entertaining the sick of any age, and it is of benefit to both you and the other person.

If every few days you are confronted by a large basket of ironing, use for prayer the time you must spend on it. Here is an example: thanksgiving for the work of scientists and the discovery of nylon and the technology of the coal and oil industries. Remember the men who work in dangerous conditions and their families. Pray for cotton workers round the world and their historically poor conditions. This could lead to contrition about the slave trade and all the misery it brought. Ask God to help us to be careful stewards of all the raw materials that we take for granted and which make our lives easier and more comfortable. You can go on to give thanks for the invention of the electric iron, and that you are physically able to do the work. Think about the electricity and textile industries and the workers involved, and so on, wherever your thoughts take you along this general line. Later you will have to learn to be more selective and not to range so far afield. After all, there will always be more ironing!

Perhaps you will prefer to take a topic from the newspapers, or something you have read about elsewhere. Thinking prayerfully about another person from their point of view may not take you very far with the facts, but even if you get them wrong it will help you to be more sympathetic and understanding and possibly more able to discern and pray for real issues. Switching off from your own concerns for a short period is in itself healthy.

If you feel that all the people who rely on you domestically create so much work that you feel it will never be done, just ask God to help you to do it as best you can. Learn to take a pride in menial tasks because for the moment that is what God is asking you to do. This is different from becoming houseproud, which is fussy and protective of the gloss. Simply take a pride in making the home a good place for people to live in and visit.

We have already recognised that retreating to a quiet place is not very practical for most of us, but if your sleep is disturbed by your own ill health or by the care of others – young babies or sick people – take half a minute to say a prayer before you go back to sleep. If you have to get out of bed to attend to someone in the middle of the night, as you push your feet into your slippers say a brief prayer for all those who work through the night so that your life can be safe and pleasant.

GOING OUT TO WORK

In some parts of the world regular 'prayer breakfasts' are popular with business people. Meeting at that time of the day means there are no disturbances and the participants face the day with a very positive attitude. This may not be possible in your business life, but bringing prayer secretly into the business dimension can make a huge difference to how you view problems at work and how you deal with people. Why not take a subject out of the job in hand for brief prayerful consideration?

Travelling time is a time of day that could be used for your prayers instead of just staring out of the window or thinking how miserable you are cooped up so closely with your fellow human beings.

PRAYING WITHOUT WORDS

In the life of a contemplative, the quiet companionship of God plays a major part. Although we may have set prayers for use at different times of the day, what is going on all the time, even during conversations, is the prayer without words. It can be tranquil or desperate, adoring or questioning, but it becomes, in time, an action akin to breathing so that we almost reach the point where we only notice it when we stop doing it, rather like holding our breath. And, like holding our breath, we have soon to stop and start praying again. Those of us who do not retire either permanently or temporarily behind monastic walls, can take the veil of prayer and carry that protection with us into our daily lives.

Our average daily life may not seem very challenging – not very like the trials suffered by the early Christians – and we may never be called on to cope with anything very dramatic, but our efforts are none the less valid. Indeed, we regularly pray (in the Lord's Prayer) that God will protect us from evil and not try out our endurance because we fear the enormity of the test against such a strong enemy as the collective evil of mankind. As contemplatives we must try to see problems in their least dramatic terms so that we do not fall into the trap of being tempted to glorify ourselves, but can deal with whatever is required of us in that part of our personality that is always tuned in to God. That is not to deny the fact that physical action may also be appropriate and, of course, our prayer life must not become so rarified that we are tempted to exclude ourselves from the very surroundings in which God has called us to function.

We may often be dissatisfied with our efforts and tempted to give up. As we mature in our prayer life we become more self critical because we are aware of excellence in the example of Christ, and the temptation to accept worldly praise for little things is great, because we so often feel we are not meeting the ideal we have set ourselves. If we are offered recognition for our deeds and there is no way of escaping without putting up a barrier of piety, then we must accept it for the sake of those who offer it; but at the same time we must guard against seeing ourselves as anything other than instruments and channels of God's purpose. To allow ourselves to be puffed up is to cut ourselves off from the thread of caring humility that we accept when we enter on the contemplative life.

Having said all this, we must always remember that we are called to appreciate, or love, ourselves in all our complexities and puzzlements. Even though we recognise our own faults we can feel we are of some worth, and through this often difficult process we can see God in the lives of others. Knowing that we are loved despite our weaknesses can help us to temper our reactions to others.

We must not delight in misery in the way we may imagine

would make us seem good and wonderful in the world's eyes but rather in the sense that God has chosen us for a particular job, has given us the comfort and support he judges we shall need, and has left space enough for the amount of misery or suffering we can therefore bear. Praise God inwardly that he sees you fit to follow a difficult path, not to your glory but to his. Then you will know you are not chosen to suffer as a punishment.

Julian of Norwich said, adapting St Paul, that we should be 'dead unto the world and alive to God'. That has been the traditional way of living a contemplative life; being literally shut away and not engaging at all in the everyday world. In her day this required some form of 'back-up team', either private servants or a community. Where the members of a contemplative order lived together there was sometimes, and still is in a few places, another adjacent order who had as part of their function the 'servicing' of the contemplatives.

In medieval times recluses might live in comparative comfort and receive visitors who in a sense served two purposes. The first was the consulting of the holy person for their own need, and the second was that for the recluses the visits acted as a safety valve for their professed life of simplicity and prayer.

There were various ways in which a contemplative could earn a living, from teaching to artistic pursuits; from keeping a few cattle to being a member of a religious order whose life was regulated by a rule. However it was organised, there were many who sought to spend most of their time in prayer despite having to cope with some of the ordinary distractions of life. It seems there were many shades of reclusiveness and many variations of lifestyle for those attempting to be contemplatives, so perhaps our own present day endeavours are not so peculiar or unlike many who have been called to this before us.

9

⚔️

YOU AND ME

How does your life as a contemplative affect your dealings with others? There is, and there must be, a 'spin off' benefit for the rest of society. By your being a more complete person and more fully used by God, those near you get the person they deserve; the whole you, both outward-looking and reflective, approachable and not an island of superior independence. A happier and more relaxed you, whose shoulders have perhaps grown broader but whose personal needs are seen to matter too; helpful and reliable but not a doormat. Someone whose life is full and demanding whatever the physical, geographical restraints, and who obviously does not entirely depend only on other people for their strength. It is possible to present a calm exterior because there is no feeling that it is necessary to compete with other people in order to prove your worth, because you already feel valued and secure. This state of mind is noticeable to those whom you meet, and may sometimes be remarked on as it makes the general atmosphere of relationships more relaxed.

Apart from praying for the people you encounter daily you will be able to meet an angry or sad face with a relaxed smile, or at least, a non-hostile expression, and anger can often be turned away and that energy used towards a constructive solution. It helps when people are facing a difficult situation to make sure that they are not also facing a

94

difficult you. This is part of the benefit that you and others enjoy from your practice of the on-going life of prayer. To be a peacemaker it is essential to spend some time in recollection and contemplation. This allows the inflamed human emotions, by which we are all governed, to settle back into perspective, and the living God's love to permeate our lives, enabling us to see life more clearly. It might be easier 'to be good' if we denied a great part of the complex mixture of chemicals, emotions and intellect that God has created in us: but we are called to use all those given attributes in his service and it is undeniably often hard.

If you are seen by others to be what the world terms a 'good person' it means that you fit their particular mental picture. What you must ask yourself is, whether you are really as good as other people think you are. You ought to be even better, for to go around making others, who are possibly also trying to live good decent lives, feel uncomfortable and ill at ease by showing a long face or a mawkishly good appearance, is not what we should be aiming for.

ENJOYING THE WORLD

We may renounce much of the world, but God wants us to enjoy it too. Not only the natural world but also the world of relationships. We have been given all sorts of instincts so that we may enjoy and support each other, physically, mentally and emotionally. If we deny this at every turn, we deny the goodness of God.

Thomas à Kempis said, 'I suggest you become more spiritual but do not despise God's goodness by despising the world.'

Creation is good, and much of what people do, make or invent is good. God works through people to reveal more of creation and we are led to increase our understanding and inventiveness. You can despise the selfishness and greed that makes us cruel and heartless and incapable of disinterested kindness, but that is different from despising the world.

CAN YOU BE BOTHERED?

Prayerful thinking must lead to some sort of action, perhaps to more prayer or to something more physical. This could take the form of a friendly act, or an allowance of time for someone. Often when I come back from shopping, the bus is full of elderly ladies, with small bags holding the few provisions needed by someone living alone. Occasionally one of them will speak to me and relate all sorts of inconsequential events and the bits and pieces of gossip which often take a much larger place in their lives now they are alone. For me, personally, it is of no great interest, but I feel that, for some of them, I may be the only person they talk to that day. Knowing that this is so often the case, I make a very conscious effort to be interested and interesting. This is not hypocrisy, but a feeling that God is allowing me to fulfil a useful purpose in that old person's life and I am grateful for that privilege.

Being dedicated to God's way and not our own means being 'bothered' to go somewhere, do something, say something, being prepared to give someone the opportunity to make contact with us. I am your opportunity to reach closer to God and you are mine. Unlike the old joke of the over-zealous boy scout, compelling old ladies to cross roads they had no intention of crossing, I must not misuse your presence in my life, but I must be ready in case our meeting holds more than just a casual acquaintance.

Through a more considered and deep prayer life our attitudes towards people and world concerns can change quite dramatically. It is not unusual for a person who has a deep prayer life to make more thoughtful contributions to church and other discussion groups, and generally to feel more willing to play an active part in the worshipping community. It does not necessarily mean a commitment to more church services, but possibly a willingness to shoulder the responsibility of some menial but vital job from which all the parish will benefit.

When you feel rather overwhelmed by life, the contemplative endeavour can help to restore your dignity and value both to you and others around you.

WORK IT OUT FOR YOURSELF

It is true that the experience of God can only be given by God himself. Your own enthusiasm cannot give God directly to anyone else. But seeing your commitment and the benefits you seem to enjoy from a particular life style could lead others to try for themselves. Once they start trying, you are out of the picture because then, their closer relationship with God has begun. If the example of someone you have met leads you to try to revolutionise your own life, remember that, by the nature of the adventure, you will be led along a different path from your friend.

WHEN ALL IS SAID AND DONE

The average life span is not long to work out our salvation, so always keep yourself in readiness to be and do what God requires of you. Try to complete each day's business on that day and always be prepared to die tomorrow. 'Let not the sun go down on your anger' is a good proverb, for it can force you to be reconciled with your adversary – who is often equally unhappy to let anger fester but finds it equally hard to make the first move. If practical actions are not possible, at least confess your sins, ask for forgiveness and state your resolve for the future. Gather to yourself the courage and consolation of God, who is waiting for you with open arms.

EXPANDING OUR IMAGE OF GOD

When we embark on a life of prayer we must expect our attitudes to be challenged and changed. The recent argument about the gender of God might lead us to feel that God is somehow a composite; having the knowledge and experience of both sides of creation. At times we feel in need of the more feminine side and at other times of the more masculine side of the Creator. This, of course, reflects our human nature, and it can be helpful some time to explore the possibilities of expanding our traditional view of God. See if you can view him as the mother creator and feel welcomed into the enfolding arms of a caring sustainer. Male and female are the human terms we understand, and at times when prayer is difficult we could sometimes be helped by expanding our view of God to encompass both genders.

I suspect that most of us, for most of the time, view God as a rather stern male. In the everyday world it is often releasing and creative for a human male to 'give in' to emotion and display what is perhaps the more feminine side of his nature. Perhaps through this sort of exercise in prayer, God is able to come closer to you, by your being willing to accept a new approach and being able to see that this does not deny your picture of him but rather enlarges and enriches it. For most of the time just stay with the image with which you are most comfortable, but remember that we are made in his own image so both male and female must be present in God the Creator.

TOGETHER IN THE KINGDOM

From Galatians chapter 3 we see that in the Kingdom of God there are no divisions between the members. The divisive labels of Jew, Greek, male and female are done away with, and we become equal members in the body of Christ; equal participants in the nature of God. The unifying love of God breaks through the barriers so that the old labels are no longer relevant.

Our physical lives are bound up with each other both in the social sense and in the sense of our industrial society and the workings of international business and trade. Without each other we just could not survive in an industrial civilisation where very few of us have enough land to support ourselves and no means of providing all the comforts and acquisitions that we so often surround ourselves with and which, indeed, form the notion of our domestic expectations.

Is it not also true that all our lives are bound together in a spiritual sense? Some realise their dependence on the prayers of others and are grateful and supportive in return. Others are not so aware but benefit anyway – but they are, in a sense, passengers in the system. How much more powerful and positive it becomes when more people, praying out of all their several varied experiences of life, join in helping to complete the web. The constant intercessions of the enclosed contemplatives are thus reinforced and expanded.

The uneventfulness of day after day of prayer when we rarely have any chance of seeing its effectiveness, can be very hard without the knowledge that we are in turn being prayed for, even down to our efforts at prayer being supported. This sort of commitment is full of risk and we may well be called on to act in ways which we can only justify to ourselves as the way we feel we are being led. The master plan is not revealed. We are only required to play our part.

It is a dangerous temptation to justify ourselves to other people by saying, 'I am called by God to do this thing', for then we are exerting a form of blackmail. God has given us our senses and intellect and expects us to use them intelligently in his service. And he is always available to us. It is we who put up the barriers and produce the dark mists of unbelief and unwillingness to be his instruments in the world.

10

SOMETHING TO THINK ABOUT

Here are some ideas to help you start your own collection which you can add to whenever you read or hear something that strikes a special note for you. I have started with the Bible and other religious books but it is probable that you will find good sources in secular literature of many different kinds. Because every collection will be very personal to the person who has made it, the best we can do for each other is to share something of what has been helpful to ourselves, by way of encouragement rather than direction.

COMFORT AND ADVICE

'Have I not commanded you? Be strong and of good courage: be not frightened, neither be dismayed; for the Lord your God is with your wherever you go' (Joshua 1.9).

'Be strong and of good courage and do it. Fear not; be not dismayed; for the Lord God, even my God is with you. He will not fail you nor forsake you until all the work for the service of the house of the Lord is finished (1 Chronicles 28.28).

'Behold you have instructed many and have strengthened the weak hands. Your words have upheld him who was stumbling and you have made firm the feeble knees. But

101

now it has come to you and you are impatient; it touches you and you are dismayed. Is not your fear of God your confidence and the integrity of your ways, your hope' (Job 4.3–4).

'Refrain from anger and forsake wrath. Fret not yourself, it tends only to evil' (Psalm 37.8).

'Cast your burden upon the Lord and he will sustain you' (Psalm 55.22).

'A soft answer turns away wrath, but a harsh word stirs up anger' (Proverbs 15.1).

'Cast all your anxieties on him, for he cares for you' (1 Peter 5.7).

'And after you have suffered a little while, the God of all grace who has called you to his eternal glory in Christ, will himself restore, establish and strengthen you' (1 Peter 5.10).

'So we do not lose heart. Though our outer nature is wasting away, our inner nature is being renewed every day. For this slight momentary affliction is preparing us for an eternal weight of glory beyond all comparison, because we look not to things that are seen but to things that are unseen; for things that are seen are transient but things that are unseen are eternal' (2 Corinthians 4.16–18).

'For you have need of endurance, so that you may do the will of God' (Hebrews 10.36).

'Rejoice always, pray constantly, give thanks in all circum-

stances; for this is the will of God in Christ Jesus for you' (1
Thessalonians 5.16).

> I'll do all the good I can
> In all the ways I can
> At all the times I can
> As long as ever I can.
>
> *A Victorian motto*

SIMPLE PRAYERS

> The God of life with guarding hold you
> The loving Christ with guarding fold you,
> The Holy Spirit, guarding, mould you,
> Each night of life to aid, enfold you,
> Each day and night of life uphold you.
> *A Gaelic prayer 'The Guarding of the God of Life'*

'Let the sea roar and all that fills it; let the field exult and
everything in it. Then shall the trees of the wood sing for joy
before the Lord for he comes to judge the earth. O give
thanks to the Lord for he is good: for his steadfast love
endures for ever' (1 Chronicles 16.32–34).

'Blessed art thou O Lord God of Israel, our father for ever
and ever. Thine O Lord is the greatness and the power and
the glory and the victory, and the majesty; for all that is in the
earth and the heavens is thine, thine is the kingdom O Lord
and thou art exalted as head above all. In thy hand are power
and might; and in thy hand is to make great and give strength
to all. And now we thank thee our God, and praise thy
glorious name' (1 Chronicles 29.10–13).

'In peace I will both lie down and sleep for thou alone, O
Lord, makes me dwell in safety' (Psalm 4.8).

'Preserve me O God, for in thee I take refuge: I have no good apart from thee' (Psalm 16.1).

'Let the words of my mouth and the meditation of my heart, be acceptable in thy sight, O Lord my rock and my redeemer' (Psalm 19.14).

'Thou hast loosed my bonds. I will offer thee the sacrifice of thanksgiving' (Psalm 116.16–17).

'Let my prayer be counted as incense before thee, and the lifting up of my hands as an evening sacrifice. Set a guard over my mouth, O Lord, keep watch over the door of my lips. Incline not my heart to any evil' (Psalm 141.2–4).

Almighty God,
who anointed Jesus at his baptism with the Holy Spirit
and revealed him as your beloved Son:
inspire us, your children,
who are born of water and the Spirit,
to surrender our lives to your service,
that we may rejoice to be called the sons of God;
through Jesus Christ our Lord.

The Collect for Epiphany

'Let us each our hearts prepare
For Christ to come and enter there'

Advent Hymn

'Do thou, O Christ, our slumbers wake;
Do thou the chains of darkness break;
Purge thou our former sins away,
And in our souls new light display.'

Hymn from the fourth century

'Maker of all to thee we pray
Fulfil in us thy joy today.'

Fifth century Easter hymn

'Christ be thou our present joy.'

From an eighth century Ascensiontide hymn

'By every power, by heart and tongue,
By act and deed, thy praise be sung.'

St Ambrose, fourth century

'Jesus, confirm my hearts desire
To work, and speak and think for thee.
Still let me guard the holy fire,
And still stir up thy gift in me.'

Charles Wesley

'Sweet Spirit, comfort me.'

Robert Herrick, seventeenth century

'Holy, Holy, Holy, Lord God of Hosts
Heaven and earth are full of your glory
Glory be to thee O Lord most high.'

ARROW PRAYERS

Lord go before me in all things.

Lord be with . . . guard, guide and comfort him/her.

Lord show me the way.

Only let your will be done in me O Lord.

NIGHT PRAYERS

The service of Compline is a beautiful one to end the day with. It can be said alone or with others in any quiet place. Alternatively, make up some prayers of your own.

There has been much wrong in me today. My heart has been cold, my thoughts have wandered, my faith has been weak. Pardon me and cleanse me from my sin and send the Holy Spirit into my soul. Take away my stony heart and strengthen me with your grace. I place myself in your hands tonight. Shelter me and keep me safe through the hours of darkness and in the morning raise me up again to your service; for Jesus Christ's sake.

Thank you Lord that in the disturbances of the night you brought clarity to my thoughts and in the morning a straight path before me.

THOUGHTS AND MEDITATIONS

'He found him in a desert land, and in the howling waste of the wilderness; he encircled him, he cared for him and he kept him as the apple of his eye. Like an eagle that stirs up its nest, that flutters over its young, spreading out its wings, catching them, bearing them on its pinions' (Deuteronomy 32.10–11).

'Let the heavens be glad and let the earth rejoice, and let them say among the nations, the Lord reigns' (1 Chronicles 16.31).

'For he is good, and his steadfast love endures forever' (2 Chronicles 5.13).

'Why is light given to him that is in misery,
and life to the bitter in soul,
Who long for death but it comes not, and dig for it more than
hid treasures;
Who rejoice exceedingly and are glad when they find the
grave.
Why is light given to a man whose way is hid,
Whom God has hedged in?
For my sighing comes as my bread and my groanings are
poured out like water.
For the thing that I fear comes upon me
I am not at ease nor am I quiet;
I have no rest but trouble comes.'
(Job 3.20–26)

'The heavens are telling the glory of God; and the Firma-
ment proclaims his handiwork' (Psalm 19.1).

'The precepts of the Lord are right, rejoicing the heart'
(Psalm 19.8).

'I waited patiently for the Lord; he inclined to me and heard
me cry. He drew me up from the desolate pit, out of the miry
bog, and set my feet upon a rock, making my steps secure.
He put a new song in my mouth, a song of praise to our God'
(Psalm 40.1–3).

Psalms 98 and 100 and many more are full of rejoicing at
creation and at the way God has upheld those sorely
afflicted.

'As you do not know how the spirit comes to the bones in the
womb of a woman with child, so you do not know the work of
God who makes everything' (Ecclesiastes 11.5).

'We are afflicted in every way, but not crushed; perplexed but not driven to despair; persecuted but not forsaken; struck down but not destroyed; always carrying in the body the death of Jesus, so that the life of Jesus may be made manifest in our bodies. For while we live we are always being given up to death for Jesus' sake' (2 Corinthians 4.8–11).

'If God is for us, who is against us? Who shall separate us from the love of Christ?' (Romans 8.31, 35).

'Lord, with thee, all things are possible' (Matthew 19.26).

'But whosoever drinks of the water I shall give him will never thirst; the water that I shall give him will turn into a spring inside him, welling up to eternal life' (John 4.14).

'God is spirit and those who worship him must worship him in spirit and truth' (John 4.24).

'Love so amazing, so divine
Demands my soul, my life, my all.'

Isaac Watts

'So shall the light that springs from thee
Be ours through all eternity.'

Fifth century hymn

'The way of the Lord is sometimes a hard bed to lie on but it is a sweet bed to die on.'

From an old monk speaking of his life

Wherever and whoever you are, you have a special place to fulfil and enjoy. Enjoyment is probably not the first word that comes to mind if you are finding life a struggle, but there are so many small blessings we have to be thankful for. Even those who are imprisoned by physical or mental circumstances can usually think of a situation worse than their own.

If you are called to a life of prayer, heartily rejoice that God has seen fit to draw from you qualities that have lain dormant during their maturing and now enable you to be ready for his service, and for a fuller life in the beautiful or difficult circumstances you are given.

Look forward to the future and never give up; God is for ever.

'Bless the Lord, O my soul; and all that is within me, bless his holy name' (Psalm 103).